Israel's Call:

How You Can Help Her Fulfill It

WHAT JEWS AND CHRISTIANS SHOULD UNDERSTAND ABOUT EACH OTHER

BY Shira Sorko-Ram

Published by Maoz, Inc.,
Box 535788, Grand Prairie, Texas 75053-5788
Used by permission.

Israel's Call: A Key To The Expansion Of The Gospel
Formerly titled, I Became as a Jew
Tenth reprint 2006. Revised edition 1991.

Printed for Maoz Inc. by Christ For The Nations Inc.
P.O. Box 769000
Dallas, Texas 75376-9000
Phone: 1-800-933-2364
Web-site: http://www.cfni.org

ISBN 0-89985-249-1

Printed in the United States of America

Unless otherwise indicated, all Scripture quotations are from the New American Standard Version of the Bible. In Scripture quotations, certain Greek-based words have been exchanged for their Hebrew-rooted equivalents.

TABLE OF CONTENTS

Section I:

A Guide to Sharing the Good News with the Jewish People

Introduction

The intention of the writer is not to offend Arab, Protestant, Catholic or Greek Orthodox, but to help those who love God to better understand Israel. The objective sought here is to break down the barriers of communication between Jew and Gentile.

> **And to the Jews I became as a Jew, so that I might win Jews; to those who are under the Law, as under the Law, though not being myself under the Law, that I might win those who are under the Law ...**
>
> **To the weak I became weak, that I might win the weak; I have become all things to all men, that I may by all means save some (I Cor. 9:20, 22).**

Among born-again believers in Jesus Christ who are closely watching for His imminent return, there is an ever-increasing concern and love for Israel and for Jewish people everywhere. The purpose of this writing is to introduce Gentile believers to the sphere of the average Jewish person and to his comprehension of Christianity. It is thereby hoped that the reader may adjust his own perspective of Judaism.

Jesus said that salvation is of the Jews (Jn. 4:22). It is generally stated that the covenant of Moses was for the Jews and that the new covenant under Jesus is for the Gentiles. But Peter, speaking to the Jews, said,

> **"It is you who are the sons of the prophets, and of the covenant which God made with your fathers, saying to Abraham, 'And in your seed all the families of the earth shall be blessed.'**

"For you first, God raised up His Servant, and sent Him to bless you by turning every one *of you* from your wicked ways" (Acts 3:25, 26).

Jesus, when He confirmed the new covenant with the cup of wine representing His blood, did so with twelve Jews. Therefore, just as the Jews received the covenant of Moses, they were also given the new covenant. It is gloriously true that the Gentiles, by the mercy of God, are also granted salvation under the new covenant or New Testament. It must be remembered, however, that the Covenant was specifically promised to the House of Israel.

"Behold, days are coming," declares the LORD, "when I will make a new covenant with the house of Israel and with the house of Judah" (Jer. 31:31).

The well-meaning Gentile who corners a Jew to tell him that Gentiles or Christians are the center of God's program will understandably receive a stony reception. Indeed, it is the Gentile who has received by grace the revelation of the God of Abraham, Isaac, and Jacob, through Jesus (a Grecian rendering of the Hebrew name *Yeshua*, the Messiah of the Jews).

The Gentile is to share with the Jews what the God of Israel has done for him, a Gentile. He who was outside the Covenant now has been brought in, only because it pleased God to do so. The Lord is merciful; it is not His will that any should perish. But the covenants were originally given to the Jewish nation. Paul explained this in Romans 11:16-18, 24:

And if the first piece *of dough* (Abraham) be holy, the lump is also; and if the root be holy, the branches are too.

But if some of the branches were broken off, and you, being a wild olive, were grafted in among them and became partaker with them of the rich root of the olive tree,

do not be arrogant toward the branches; but if you are arrogant, *remember that* it is not you who supports the root, but the root *supports* you. ...

For if you were cut off from what is by nature a wild olive tree, and were grafted contrary to nature into a cultivated olive tree, how much more shall these who are the natural *branches* be grafted into their own olive tree?

What Jews Know About Christians

Many Christians think of Jewish people as people who do not know God. The Gentile should realize that a Jew's conception of a Christian is also a person without God — that is, the true God of Israel.

Some Jewish perceptions of Christianity are perhaps more valid than the Christian comprehension of Judaism; others are clearly misconceptions.

The Jewish understanding of a Christian is anybody and everybody who is born in the Western world and is not a Jew or a Muslim (or Hindu, Buddhist, etc.). A Jew believes someone is a Christian because he is born a Christian, just as someone is a Muslim because he is born a Muslim. Anyone born in the United States, Canada, South America or Europe is presumed to be a Christian — except for those born a Jew or Muslim. Columbus, Billy Graham, the Pope, Marilyn Monroe, Hitler and you (if you are not a Jew, Muslim, etc.) are all considered Christians.

This does not mean that Jews feel all Christians are to be despised. Israelis usually tend to measure a Christian's goodness by his attitude toward the Jews. Danes, who helped save so many Jews during World War II, are considered good Christians; and the Germans, who slaughtered the Jews, are considered bad Christians. Many times the Israelis have referred to certain public figures as "righteous Gentiles" because of their attitude toward the preservation of Israel.

The non-Jew should be aware that the Hebrew word for Gentile or nation is *goy*. The word in Hebrew for heathen and pagan is also *goy*. In Old Testament times, Israel worshiped God, but neighboring nations — or the heathen — did not know Him.

It logically follows that the religions of the Gentiles (heathen) are heathen religions, or at least inferior to Judaism. The semantic development is understandable. The connotation has been carried down to the present day. Any Jew knows some heathen religions are idolatrous and some are not. For example, the Muslim religion is in no sense idolatrous. One may walk into any mosque in the world, and he will never see a graven image or likeness (picture). But the Jew understands Christianity to be not only a Gentile or heathen religion, but also an idolatrous heathen religion. An Israeli could take you into almost any cathedral in Israel and point out to you what he considers graven images — a violation of the Ten Commandments. This was one of the very sins his ancestors committed and, as a result, were carried off into Babylonian captivity.

Watching ancient Romans worship in their temples before the gods of Venus and Mars, or observing Christians in a church praying before statues or pictures creates precisely the same impression on a Jew.

The Three Great Religions

The Israeli sees his own country split into the three main religions, and he considers the fruits of each. The Jews are of the Jewish religion, the Arabs are either Christian or Muslim. Among the Arabs as a whole, there is not a great deal of difference between a Muslim's and a Christian's hatred of the Jew. Both Christian and Muslim Arabs have determined to throw Israel into the sea.

One of the oldest organizations of Arab terrorists — which have carried out terrorist acts for several decades — owes its formation to a self-acclaimed Marxist who also regards himself to be a Christian. One can often read in the Jerusalem papers statements such as the following: "Joseph Saalim, Christian Arab, killed one Israeli and wounded two others in a hand grenade attack against a moving car. ..." Active terrorism is a part of the life of both Christian and Muslim Arabs. At times, even clerical leaders have been known to aid terrorists.

Both Muslim and Christian Arabs are fiercely proud of their religions. Notwithstanding a few fine exceptions, Christian Arabs are no more cognizant of the new birth than Muslim Arabs. This lack of spiritual understanding is not limited, of course, to Arabs. Can one say any more of the millions in the Christian nations of France, Germany or South America? And what about the Christians in America who are considered heathen in God's sight, regardless of the name they attach to themselves? Of course, a few Arabs have encountered the God of Israel through Jesus, the Son of God, just as a few French, etc., have. But in surveying Christendom as a whole, the true followers of Christ are a small minority in any country; certainly this is true in Arab countries.

Christian Arabs are highly suspicious of anyone, be he Muslim or Jew, who has converted to Christianity. In fact, many Arab Christians would look with disdain on such a person. To them it is a matter of tradition and family ties. Why would a Muslim want to become a Christian? Unthinkable! And a Jew who joins the ranks of Arab Christians would be a mystery indeed! Since each Muslim, Christian and Jew owes much to his family, nation and traditions, crossing over from one religion to another is unacceptable. Meanwhile, the message of salvation and the knowledge of a living God, Who abides in every human being desiring Him, are virtually unknown.

I overheard a conversation between a lovely American tourist and a young Arab from Jerusalem. The Arab, a local hairdresser, happened to be a man of exceedingly low morals. The lady asked him in the best evangelical manner, "Are you a Christian?" He replied, "Oh, yes!" She answered, "Oh, I'm so happy to come halfway around the world and meet a Christian here. Thank the Lord!" The hairdresser was beaming. He was pleased that she was pleased about his being a Christian. Of course, neither one knew what the other was saying. She was talking about a spiritual experience; he, a cultural background.

Christian Persecution of the Jews

The reader may find it regrettable that Arabs give such a poor example of true Christianity to Jews. But the Jew finds nothing incongruous about the Arab attitude at all. Each Israeli child learns in school that his history is one long, tragic persecution of Jews by Christians. Anti-Semitism has always been present in the Christian world to some extent, but at certain points in history it has been vicious. For example, during the Crusades, Christian hordes swarmed across Europe toward the Holy Land, slaughtering the Jews as they advanced. One such incident happened in Esslingen, Germany. There the Crusaders locked all Jews in the village inside the local synagogue and burned it down. The Crusade period was a very dark time in Jewish history.

Another unspeakable tragedy occurred in Spain. During the period of Muslim rule in Spain, the Jews were left alone. A Jewish diaspora culture advanced to an all-time high. However, when the Christian King Ferdinand and Queen Isabella united Spain under their throne in the 15th century, they began a horrific persecution of the Jews. The Jewish people were told, "Kiss the cross and become a Christian." The alternative was deportation. Thousands were tortured and killed. Most, feeling they could not become a part of an idolatrous heathen religion, preferred death or expulsion. Some took oaths of Christianity, but were deported anyway.

In Russia, persecution took the form of pogroms. For centuries under the Christian czars, the Russian army swept through Jewish villages to slaughter, rape and destroy. At times, Russian soldiers — or others with some spark of feeling toward the Jews — warned them to flee before the army arrived. Countless Jewish villages throughout Russia and Eastern Europe received orders that Jews would no longer be able to reside there. So the Jewish people would pack up their belongings, put them in carts and start down the road, not knowing where they were going.

It is not accidental that many of the first Jews to return in this century to the Holy Land came from Russia and Eastern Europe. Although what was then called Palestine was a land of malarial swamps and desert wastes, Jews preferred it to continual ejection from places in Christendom.

The culmination of all persecutions was masterminded by Hitler. Since Hitler was neither a Jew nor a Muslim, he was, in the eyes of Jews, a Christian. (He had a Catholic background.) If a questioning Christian Gentile strongly resists the idea that Hitler was a Christian, the Jew will answer that Hitler did not destroy these millions of Jews by himself. Thousands of Germans, Poles and others who called themselves Christians herded Jews onto the trains or met them at the sites of destruction. If you should have opportunity to look through old World War II pictures, notice the Crusaders' Cross pinned to the Nazi uniform. The cross is the symbol of Christianity to the Jews.

Even today, Jewish people in such countries as France rarely discuss with a Gentile the fact that they are Jews. And in the Passover season of 1970, European papers published reports that Jews had been accused (as they have for centuries) of killing Gentile children for their blood to be used at the Passover.

Communism has collapsed. And at this moment, the old line churches — Russian Orthodox in the Soviet Union, Catholic in Poland and Eastern Europe — have come out into the open. Anti-Semitism is again rapidly gaining ground, causing Jews living there to fear for their lives. There is also a visible growth in hatred of the Jews in Catholic and Protestant Western Europe, Scandinavia, Britain, and even parts of the U.S.

Now imagine a sincere, born-again American or European traveling to Israel. He finds himself caught up in the ecstasy of the reborn land, with its rich promises of God for Israel, and he asks a Jew, "Wouldn't you like to become a Christian?" The Jew's negative response inevitably leaves both parties puzzled.

Thus the paradox: the positive, but meaningless answer from a Christian Arab, who is glad to tell you he is a Christian, and the extremely negative reaction from a Jew. The Jew understands the question thus: "Would you like to become a part of a Gentile, idolatrous religion which consists of heathen who have tried to exterminate the Jews for nearly 2,000 years?" The Jew, at best, will probably politely answer, "I cannot be a traitor to my people."

Other Problems in Semantics

The word *church* in the New Testament has a different meaning than that ascribed to it today by most Christians. In the New Testament, *church* never meant *building*. The word meant *an assembly, group or community of believers* — the veritable body of Christ. Wherever human beings were with the indwelling God, there was the Church. When Paul wrote to the Church at Ephesus, he was certainly not writing to a building, but rather the little assemblies throughout the city which comprised the Church. The same connotation is found in the term *church in the wilderness*. Moses led the community of believers (i.e., Israel) through the wilderness.

But the Jew associates the word *church* with an idolatrous, heathen temple. For that reason, most Jews do not wish to visit a church.

Missionary is one of the most hated words in Hebrew. The Jewish person reasons as follows: "The Christians have tried to exterminate us for 2,000 years. Finally, we have found our way back to our own land with God's help, and what happens? The Christians follow right after us and tell us we should not be Jews anymore. We should convert to Christianity." The Jew feels this is an attempt to exterminate the Jewish race, and that it is as deadly as any form ever used. Occasionally, when an Israeli did become a born-again believer, he also, unfortunately, learned how to be a good Western Christian. Bacon and eggs began to taste better than gefilte fish. Soon he felt foreign to his land and his people. He, therefore, asked to immigrate to the United States or Europe.

Incidentally, Messianic Jews in Israel have substituted the word *shaliach* (pronounced shah-LEE-ah, with a guttural "h" on the last syllable) for the term *missionary*. *Shaliach* means a "sent one" and, in modern Hebrew, refers to an ambassador, emissary or delegate. In the New Testament, *shaliach* is the only appropriate word available in Hebrew to translate the Greek word for apostle.

To a Jewish person, **convert** means to turn his back on his nation, people, God and Scriptures and become a part of a Gentile religion. Thus, the term **converted Jew** is an anathema.

This connotation of **convert** is certainly not based on Scripture. The King James version of the Bible uses the word **convert** in place of the exact Hebrew and Greek words meaning repent. (The meaning of this word is more fully considered later.) For example, the phrase in Matthew 18:3, "... Except ye be converted ..." is more properly rendered "unless you repent." In many modern versions of the Old and New Testaments, **convert** is replaced by the closer meaning **repent**.

I would never use the word **convert** to a Jew, because he does not know the King James meaning of the word. Paul said that if meat offended his brother, he would eat no meat as long as the world stands (I Cor. 8:13). Surely we, upon realizing how a Jew understands this word, will not use it to confuse him and hinder him from finding God. I would hate to think that I kept someone from the Kingdom of God because of my vocabulary.

In the sense that the Jewish person understands the word, he certainly must not convert — that is, stop being a Jew and go over to another religion. He must instead turn around and go back to the God of his fathers that he has left.

Furthermore, many Jews who have converted to nominal Christianity, usually to marry, have rarely repented of their sins. So, the meaning is further muddled. On the other hand, a believing Jew or Messianic Jew is one who has repented.

The Phrase, "The Jews Rejected Christ"

Many times when a Gentile speaks to a Jew of spiritual things, he sees the Jew as one of those who rejected Christ — with all it implies. The answer to that, of course, is: "Did the Gentiles as a whole accept Christ?" An overwhelming, tragic "no"! What percentage of Gentiles, even those of the Western world, has accepted Jesus as Savior and Lord of their lives? The percentage is small. In many countries, one would have to search far and wide to find even a few born-again believers. The truth is, man has rejected God; and Jesus died because of, and for, all mankind.

A Jew without salvation is no different from a Chinese, American or any other Gentile without salvation. If he is lost, he is no more lost than the liberal or fundamental churchman who claims a name without the reality. All mankind stands naked before God; in great compassion and love He has offered redemption to all. The message for today's Jewish person is:

"Comfort, O comfort My people," says your God.

"Speak kindly to Jerusalem; And call out to her, that her warfare has ended, that her iniquity has been removed, that she has received of the Lord's hand Double for all her sins" (Isa. 40:1, 2).

Although we know the time of Jacob's trouble is yet to come upon Israel, indeed upon all the earth, we are assured also that the time of Israel's redemption is near. And to every Gentile believer filled with the love of God, those verses speak straight to his heart.

The Meaning of Christ

Two more observations may be noted concerning Christianity:

1. **Every believer is interested in the meaning *or* idea *conveyed by the Scriptures rather than specific* words.**

We all consider ourselves *witnesses* for our Lord. And we know that the name of our God is *Jehovah*.

Yet, unless we belong to that particular sect, we do not tell people we are Jehovah's Witnesses. Even so, the term is technically correct for all believers. Likewise, all believers belong to the Church of God. Yet, a believer may say, "No, I am not Church of God, but a Baptist." So, believers relate words to specific meanings. They use or do not use them according to the meaning they convey.

In the same way then, a believer should know that when he asks a Jew to become a Christian, the Jew will understand the question as, "Would you like to become a member of an idolatrous, heathen, Jew-persecuting religion?" The believer would best not ask that question. (It may be argued from the Scriptures that only Gentiles were called Christians or Messianics in New Testament days.)

2. **Christian *comes from the word* Christ. *The English word* Christ *has its roots in the Greek (a Gentile) language.***

If one would ask the average Jew what *Christ* means, he would have no idea. Actually, the concept of *Christ* did not originate with the Greeks. It is found in the Hebrew Scriptures. The Hebrew word for *Christ* is *Messiah*.

I could not appreciate a man telling me about the English word *Christ* if I only understood Chinese. Although he might be explaining the concept correctly, I simply would not understand him. So, a Jewish person from a Hebrew background could have no appreciation of the word *Christ*; and because it has no meaning, it can have no relationship with his needs or problems.

But any Jewish person whether he agrees with one's theology or not, knows that the word *Messiah* — Anointed One — signifies a coming deliverer, the redeemer of Israel. Although he would not know what the English word *Jesus* means, he would understand when told that Jesus' Hebrew name is Yeshua, meaning salvation (see pages 16-17 for further explanation). The Jewish person would at least understand the concept of Yeshua the Messiah.

Just as no one ever asks a Gentile if he would like to accept Yeshua as his Messiah, one should never ask a Jew if he wants to accept Jesus Christ. Yeshua (Jesus) is, first of all, the Messiah of the Jews.

The Gentile believer might counter that Galatians 3:28 states that "There is neither Jew nor Greek ... in Christ Jesus." It is true that all men need God, and all men, without distinction, may have access to God through His Son. But the same Scripture says there is neither male nor female — also true. In the Messiah both have equal access to God. But just as male and female exist, so do Jew and non-Jew. Nearly every Gentile I have ever met wished to remain a Gentile. Likewise, almost every Jew most emphatically wants to remain a Jew.

I do not pretend to have all the answers concerning God's plan for His nation, Israel; but the Scriptures do reveal that God, Who has nearly overturned heaven and earth to preserve the Jewish people for 2,000 years, has not done so merely to bring them back to Israel so that they could become Gentiles.

> **"If this fixed order [the sun, moon and stars] departs from before Me," declares the LORD, "Then the offspring of Israel also shall cease from being a *nation* before Me forever"** (Jer. 31:36 emphasis mine).

Why Shouldn't a Christian Train Jewish People to Say "Jesus Christ"?

The whole idea of Messiah, the Anointed One, is Jewish in origin. Yeshua said, "... salvation is from the Jews" (Jn. 4:22). No other people or religion has ever conceived of a son-redeemer sent by his father to save the world.

Furthermore, when Yeshua was born, the angel told Miriam (Mary) to call the child "Yeshua." As the boy grew, He answered to the name *Yeshua* — not the English equivalent of Jesus or that of any other language. There was literally no other name except Yeshua!

So when the first Jewish believers went into non-Jewish regions, they had to bring these Jewish concepts and Hebrew names into a pagan world. One tool that greatly helped them was the Septuagint — the Greek translation of the Old Testament. The Septuagint was used by the Greek-speaking Jewish community scattered throughout the Hellenistic world.

The Septuagint translators sometimes encountered a word that, being rooted in a Jewish concept, had no Greek equivalent. For example, they "greekized" *Maschiach* (found in Daniel) in order to make it more familiar to the Greek-speaking Jews and easier to pronounce. They decided to literally translate the concept "Anointed One" into its Greek equivalent. The word that was created was *Christos* — a "native" Greek word that was understood by non-Hebrew speakers.

As Jewish believers like Paul began to spread the Good News to the pagan Greek world, they keenly felt the necessity to "greekize" many more Hebrew words which were based on Jewish concepts.

God is a universal God, they reasoned, and Yeshua is the Lamb of God Who came to take away the sin of the world. Why then cause a stumbling block by preserving Hebrew-sounding names? Why not convert them to words which had meaning and were familiar to Greek people?

The same process obviously occurred with the Hebrew name "Yeshua." It certainly didn't sound Greek, didn't look Greek and was probably difficult for Greek-speakers to pronounce. Certain disciples of Yeshua, who were crying out to God for the souls of the pagan men and women, felt it expedient to allow these people to easily and comfortably pronounce Yeshua's name. Result: *Iesous*.

In this "greekized" form, therefore, *Iesous Christos* was preached throughout the known world. The name of the Messiah was further adapted into various languages beyond the Greek-speaking communities. Jesus Christ in English, Jesu Christo in Spanish, and Jesus Christus in German are but a few of the adaptations found in the Western languages alone. Other examples of English adaptations include: Lord (Adonai), Passover (Pesach), Mosaic Law or Pentateuch (Torah), Sabbath, a day of rest (Shabbat).

Never in their wildest dreams, however, did early Jewish evangelists consider preaching to the Jews about Iesous Christos. This was against the principle and spirit by which they adapted Yeshua's name to the Gentile languages. The early believers understood that the truths of the Gospel are to be preached in the vernacular, the language and the understanding of the person being reached.

> **So also you, unless you utter by the tongue speech that is clear, how will it be known what is spoken? For you will be speaking into the air (I Cor. 14:9).**

Even though the context of this Scripture is completely different, the principle of speaking to be understood applies to every situation.

Those who truly love the Jewish people will find a way to "speak clearly" so as not to speak into the air. They will find a way to communicate rather than expect the unsaved Jew to "understand" the real and original meaning of "greekized" words. "Gentilized" words may be precious to the one witnessing, but they are usually meaningless, or worse yet, may arouse negative associations within the Jewish heart.

If men have adapted the name of Yeshua HaMashiach to hundreds of languages, should not the Jewish people be free to use the original name of the King of the Jews? In being all things to all men, you will be following in the footsteps of Paul, the Jewish apostle to the Gentiles, and other like-minded early ambassadors.

What is a Jew?

One of the greatest problems facing Jews today is, "Who exactly is a Jew?" The government of Israel has finally decided that a Jew is one whose mother is a Jewess, or who has been officially converted. But as for the question of what really makes a Jew a Jew, no one seems to know.

To find the answer one must go to the place of the word's origin — the Bible. The word *Jew* originally was a name for those who were from the tribe of Judah. Judah was the son of Jacob, the son of Isaac, the son of

Abraham. Abraham and his posterity were separated from the heathen through a covenant with God. God called Abraham His friend. Abraham communicated, worshiped and fellowshiped with God. To him, God was a personal acquaintance. Jehovah made rich promises to Abraham. In return, Abraham listened for his Lord's commands, instructions and ordinances. And Abraham obeyed. He proved that his trust was total when he was ready to give to God the thing he loved most: his son.

Abraham, the father of Israel, became God's chosen because of his spiritual relationship; he daily listened for and daily obeyed the voice of God. It is not to be implied that Abraham understood all the mysteries of the future. He knew little of God's plan of redemption. He simply told Isaac, "God will provide." He did not even know about the Law of Moses to come; but without qualification, he obeyed God and trusted Him to fulfill His will. Abraham is the biblical example of a true Jew. A man of less faith is an incomplete Jew.

How Does a Jew Encounter the Messiah, the Redeemer of Israel?

How does one become a Messianic Jew? (We will now use the Hebrew terms instead of the Greek.) The Scriptures, of course, give the answer. The message of the prophets was clear and unfailingly the same: REPENT. The Hebrew word for repent is *shuv*. It means to *turn around, turn back*. In other words, stop, turn around and go back to your God whom you have left. It not only means to be sorry, but also to turn in the opposite direction and proceed. Every prophet had virtually the same message. Ezekiel 33:11 is but an example:

> **"Say to them, 'As I live!' declares the LORD GOD, 'I take no pleasure in the death of the wicked, but rather that the wicked turn from his way and live. Turn back, turn back from your evil ways! Why then will you die, O house of Israel?'"**

The necessity of this message is understood when the concept of sin is understood. Sin is doing what one desires instead of what pleases God. Everyone is a sinner. David said, "... There is no one who does good ..." (Psa. 14:3).

When John the Baptist appeared, his message was identical: "Repent, for the kingdom of heaven is at hand" (Matt. 3:2). The Greek basis for this New Testament word *repent* means a turning of one's mind, while the Hebrew emphasizes a turning of the heart. Both are necessary. After Yeshua was tested in the wilderness, the Bible records that His very first public sermon began with, "Repent, for the kingdom of heaven is at hand" (Matt. 4:17). Repentance is preparation for salvation.

The second step is to believe in Yeshua. Someone cannot believe in Yeshua until he has first repented. Thus, John had to prepare the way for Yeshua. The Western world is full of Christians who believe in Jesus but have never repented of their sins. These Gentiles may be described as heathen Christians — the opposite of born-again Christians.

To believe in Yeshua, a Jew must first become acquainted with Him. The most obvious step is to read about His life and teachings in the first four books of the New Testament. Also, the Book of Hebrews, Paul's special epistle to the Jews, will give a better understanding of Yeshua and His mission to the Jews.

Before one can truly believe in Yeshua, he must change the direction of his life and turn toward God. But why believe in Yeshua? In English, the meaning of Jesus' name is lost, for Jesus is not a name like Joe or Robert or Jack. As we have explained, *Jesus* means *savior* or *salvation* in Hebrew. Thus, the Scripture could be translated:

And she shall bring forth a son, and thou shalt call his name *Salvation* **(Yeshua): for he shall** *save* **(yoshia) his people from their sins (Matt. 1:21 KJV).**

Thus *Yeshua* and *yoshia* are both forms of the Hebrew word that means *save*.

And there is salvation in no one else; for there is no other name under heaven that has been given among men, by which we must be saved (Acts 4:12).

Yeshua took on Himself the very name *Salvation*. Most Hebrew-speaking people don't even know His correct name and are surprised to hear the real pronunciation and meaning. Many will not believe His name is Yeshua until shown in a Hebrew New Testament. A Jewish believer is readily identifiable by the way he pronounces Yeshua's name in Hebrew — a significant witness.

An Orthodox Jew might counter, "But the Messiah has to be the ruler of the earth. Our Scriptures contain many promises that the Messiah will bring peace to earth."

> **"Behold, the days are coming," declares the LORD, "when I will fulfill the good word which I have spoken concerning the house of Israel and the house of Judah.**
>
> **"In those days and at that time I will cause a righteous Branch of David to spring forth; and He shall execute justice and righteousness on the earth.**
>
> **"In those days Judah shall be saved, and Jerusalem shall dwell in safety; and this is *the name* by which she shall be called: the LORD is our righteousness." (Jer. 33:14-16).**
>
> **For a child will be born to us, a son will be given to us; and the government will rest on His shoulders; ... There will be no end to the increase of His government or of peace, on the throne of David and over His Kingdom ... (Isa. 9:6, 7).**
>
> **Then it will come about in that day that the nations will resort to the root of Jesse, Who will stand as a signal for the peoples; and His resting place will be glorious (Isa. 11:10).**

The simple answer is, of course, that Yeshua the Messiah is coming the second time to do just that. But the Jewish people in Israel, for the most part, have never heard that Christians believe Yeshua is coming back. The historic churches have tended to emphasize only that He came to earth, died and left. To hear that some people's lives are centered around the expected return of Yeshua the Messiah has come as somewhat of a shock to many Jews.

The Christian who is not expecting Him to return is simply telling the Jew that Yeshua cannot be the Messiah. He then will have to be someone else, because the Messiah promised in the Scriptures must come to rule the earth from the throne of David in the city of Jerusalem.

The next logical question is: If Yeshua really is the Messiah, *when* is He coming back? This is a valid question; it was asked by the Jews who followed Yeshua when He was in Israel nearly 2,000 years ago. Yeshua's answer is recorded in Luke 21 and Matthew 24. Before going into these chapters, let us imagine the place and the time of Yeshua's departure from the earth. It is New York today. Yeshua is standing, talking to twelve New Yorkers. He has told them that He is going to leave New York, but at the end of the age, He will come back. They ask Him when this will occur.

Yeshua answers the following: "New York is going to be destroyed. The huge skyscrapers will be demolished, without one stone being left on another. All of the residents of New York will be scattered throughout the world. Many will be killed and New York will be in alien hands. Then one day, New Yorkers will begin returning to New York, and the city will actually come back into their possession. When these things take place, know that I, Yeshua, will come back. In fact, I will return in that very generation."

If you were listening to that conversation, what would you think? You would probably say, "Well, He certainly made it clear and definite as to the time He is coming back." Now let us look at the words of Jesus:

> **And He answered and said to them, "Do you not see all these things? Truly I say to you, not one stone here shall be left upon another, which will not be torn down"** (Matt. 24:2).

Then speaking of the Jews, He said,

> **"... and they will fall by the edge of the sword, and will be led captive into all the nations; and Jerusalem will be trampled underfoot by the Gentiles until the times of the Gentiles be fulfilled ..."** (Lk. 21:24)

This verse was literally fulfilled in June, 1967. And all prophecies concerning the Jews' return to the Land and subsequent turning back to God must be fulfilled. For Yeshua said,

> "... not the smallest letter or stroke shall pass away
> from the Law, until all is accomplished" (Matt. 5:18).

> And then will they see THE SON OF MAN COMING IN A CLOUD
> with power and great glory (Lk. 21:27).

Yeshua went on to say that when the fig tree (a symbol of political
Israel) put forth its leaves, summer would be nigh.

> Even so you too, when you see all these things,
> recognize that He is near, *right* at the door (Matt. 24:33;
> see also Lk. 21:31, 32).

Then, to re-emphasize the weight of His words, He added:

> Truly I say to you, this generation will not pass away
> until all these things take place (Matt. 24:34).

I will tell any Jew that I am looking for Yeshua's return in this
generation.

The Times of the Jews

Peter was a Jew. He came to know God through Yeshua, the Messiah
of Israel. Peter served Yeshua; he followed Him; he watched Him die; he
saw Him go to heaven. Afterward, Peter went with the other disciples
to an upper room, and he received the Holy Spirit. Soon he was
preaching to thousands of Jews. He became a pillar in the congregation
of believers at Jerusalem. Ten years came and went, yet one important
truth had escaped him. Peter did not know that *Gentiles* could also find
redemption in the God of Abraham, Isaac and Jacob.

This does not mean Peter thought all Gentiles were doomed to be
eternally lost. He merely thought that for a Gentile to become entitled
to God's promises, he must first become a Jew.

Why did Peter think that? Not because he was unintelligent or spiritually
obtuse. Virtually every other Jewish believer believed the same thing.
God had dealt with the Gentiles thus for several thousand years. How
did Rahab, a citizen of Jericho, find her salvation? She proved her belief
in the God of Israel by physically joining that nation. Likewise, Ruth, the
Moabitess, became an Israelite and even an ancestor of King David.

It took a shocking vision from heaven to persuade Peter to preach to a Gentile family (Cornelius'). He was again surprised when he saw them respond. Peter was finally convinced when he actually saw these non-Jews receiving the Holy Spirit (Acts 10).

Until this time Peter's message was, "Would you like to become a born-again Jew?"

On the other hand, Paul — a Jew — was called by God specifically to the Gentiles. All his life he fought the tendency of the Jewish believers to think of themselves as the only group of people to whom salvation was given. *It was understood by all, of course, that Jews still received salvation as Jews* (See Acts 21:24). But Paul maintained that to receive salvation Gentiles should become simply believing Gentiles. A "gentilized" term — *Christian* — was even coined from the Hebrew concept of followers of Messiah or Messianics.

The death of Yeshua around A.D. 30 had marked the end of the times of the Jews, or the time when one had to become a Jew to find God. For 40 years, Jewish believers — who were mostly in and around Jerusalem — continued in their Messianic faith. Gentiles, on the other hand, without taking on Jewish tradition, accepted *Iesous* (the Greek spelling of Jesus) as Lord and Savior, and continued to follow their Greek culture.

Then came the destruction of Jerusalem in A.D. 70. And the times of the Gentiles, which actually began with the death of Yeshua, emerged in its fullness after 40 years. The times of the Jews, which actually began to ebb with the captivities, heard its death knell with the crucifixion of Yeshua. It finally came to a total halt with the destruction of Jerusalem.

Thereafter, Jews were scattered throughout the world. Any Jew who accepted Yeshua almost invariably became a Gentile; that is, his children were raised as Gentiles, and his grandchildren no longer thought of themselves as Jews. It was an exact reverse of the times of the Jews when Ruth, Rahab and many others joined themselves to the Jews in order to serve God. Speaking as God's mouthpiece, Moses hinted at the phenomenon of the Gentiles:

They have made Me jealous with *what* is not God; they

have provoked Me to anger with their idols. So I will make them jealous with *those who* are not a people; I will provoke them to anger with a foolish nation (Deut. 32:21).

If God's Word is to be taken literally, the times of the Gentiles can be said to have ended in 1967 with the Jewish recapture of the Old City of Jerusalem. However, since God's times always gradually fade (instead of cutting off at a second's notice), we may be assured that God will continue to deal with the Gentiles a short time longer — just as He did with the Jews for 40 years after the death of the Messiah. The move of God's grace began to deal in ever more powerful waves with the Gentiles as Gentiles after A.D. 30. Likewise, God has begun to bring Jews into repentance and faith as Jews. Why? Because the times of the Jews are once more upon us, and will continue to expand until His coming. And just as God has faithfully fulfilled His revealed will until now, so will He continue to fulfill it.

As far as I know, almost every Jew who accepted Yeshua into his life before the recapture of Jerusalem also claimed allegiance to the Gentile peoples. After June, 1967, a constantly increasing number of Jews have been redeemed by the blood of Yeshua, the Jewish Messiah, as members of the Jewish faith.

Hebrew Christians

In no way does this berate those Jews who became, in a lesser or greater sense, Gentile Christians or Hebrew Christians. After all, it is not a sin to be a Gentile! The time of the Gentiles, when believing Jews generally had to find their spiritual direction from born-again Gentiles continued until June, 1967.

How wonderful that Ruth the Moabitess became a Jewess when she accepted the God of Israel during the times of the Jews. But later, when the time of the Gentiles arrived, Paul discouraged the Gentiles from becoming Jews.

It is interesting to note that only after June, 1967, did I meet Jews who accepted Yeshua the Messiah without declaring themselves Christians. Other Jews who have known the Lord for longer periods find themselves moving back into identity with their people and their ancient faith.

Until the last few years, almost all Jews (with some outstanding exceptions) who became Hebrew Christians were peripheral Jews — Jews who had only loose ties with their heritage and their religion. I am looking for the day when traditional rabbis will stand up in their synagogues and proclaim the Good News of the Kingdom — just as happened in the days of the early apostles.

To be blunt, a Jew does not want to be a good member of the Assemblies of God, a good Baptist or a good Anglican. He wants to know how to be a good Jew — a believing Jew.

Religions that are based on organizations must fade into the background. The truth is, there is only one true faith. In the strictest sense, it is the Jewish faith (as opposed to religion), the faith given to the house of Israel through Abraham. The faith that brought with it the promise of the Messiah and redemption of the world. The Jew must return to this faith, which will bring him all the salvation God has promised him. He does not need to convert to a new religion or set of traditions. No religion — neither his nor anyone else's — can save. The Jew has plenty of traditions, some difficult, some beautiful. It is certainly not necessary to throw one's traditions completely overboard. Does an American stop celebrating Thanksgiving or the Fourth of July because he becomes born-again? But neither can traditions save. Only Yeshua can save.

> **"... for there is no other name under heaven that has been given among men, by which we must be saved"** **(Acts 4:12).**

And that includes names of churches, synagogues, organizations, phraseology and slogans.

There is only one name that a Jew must accept: Yeshua.

Section II: Questions Often Discussed When Sharing With Jewish People

Did the Jews Crucify Christ?

This is one of the most sensitive issues of all between Jew and Christian. Satan, knowing that only Yeshua, the Son of God, can redeem the Jewish people, concentrated his efforts on making Yeshua a name that is an anathema to the Jewish people. How did he accomplish this?

While Yeshua was on earth, He was adored and worshiped by large crowds of Jewish people. The New Testament plainly says this. For instance, when Yeshua came into Jerusalem a week before His death, all of Jerusalem was stirred towards Him (Jn. 12:12, 13).

But the religious leaders, jealous of His popularity and power and enraged because Yeshua was calling these self-righteous leaders to repentance, decided to kill Him.

> **But the chief priests took counsel that they might put Lazarus to death also; because on account of him many of the Jews were going away, and were believing in Yeshua (Jn. 12:10, 11).**

> **"If we let Him go on like this, all men will believe in Him ..." (Jn. 11:48).**

The religious leaders were afraid to arrest Yeshua during Passover. Thousands of Jewish people who believed in — or at least were sympathetic to — Yeshua were gathered in Jerusalem. The leaders knew they must seize Him secretly.

> **But they were saying, "Not during the festival, lest a riot occur among the people" (Matt. 26:5).**

And so they came by night, imprisoned Him and sentenced Him to death. The Jews condemned Him, the Gentiles crucified Him. So who should be blamed? To that, Yeshua gave the most incredible answer:

> "I am the good shepherd; the good shepherd lays down His life for the sheep. ... No one has taken it away from Me, but I lay it down on My own initiative. I have authority to lay it down, and I have authority to take it up again. This commandment I received from My Father" (Jn. 10:11, 18).

Why did He do it? We all know the answer to that:

> But He was pierced through for *our* transgressions, He was crushed for our iniquities ... (Isa. 53:5).

He didn't have to do it. He could have let us all die in our sins! But He chose to die for the sins of the world. He died for sinners. Each and every sinner was the cause of His death. That means *me*!

Yes, it is true that the Jewish people from whom Yeshua came were tested and found to be an evil and unregenerate people. What does that indicate about the rest of the world?

In a small, poor, mountain town in the southern part of the United States, the entire population became ill with a stomach disorder. State authorities came to investigate the cause. They took back with them a test tube full of the town's well water. In their laboratories, they found the water heavily polluted. Returning to the well, they discovered a sow and her baby pigs had drowned at the bottom.

The government authorities did not have to take *all* the water from the well to test for water pollution; they only had to take a sample. The Jewish people were the sample for God's test tube. Testing a small percentage of humanity, God found mankind utterly polluted. The Holy Spirit, through Paul, stated it thus:

> Now we know that whatever the Law says, it speaks to those (the Jews) who are under the Law, that every mouth may be closed, and all the world (all the Gentiles and Jews) may become accountable to God (Rom. 3:19).

Whatever guilt the Jewish leaders who condemned Him bore, Yeshua took care of it.

**"Father, forgive them; for they know not what they do"
... (Lk. 23:34, KJV).**

Does God, or does God not, answer Yeshua's prayers?

Yeshua said if we do not forgive, God will not forgive us! We must forgive the Jews for initiating Yeshua's death — just as we must forgive the Gentiles for executing Him. If He had not died, we could not be saved!

For many hundreds of years, Satan has used so-called Christians to taunt and terrorize the Jews with, "You Christ killers! You are cursed because you killed Christ!"

Often this has been a Jew's first introduction to Yeshua. Many times these insults have been thrown at Jewish children who did not even know the meaning of the venomous insult. The devil, knowing that Yeshua is the only hope for the nation of Israel, was determined that His Name would be associated with horror and repugnance.

Yeshua came, not to condemn the world, but that the world through Him might be saved (Jn. 3:17). The Spirit of Messiah will comfort the Jewish people. The spirit of the devil will crush.

Why Do Jews Have Problems with the Concept of Trinity?

To a Jewish person, the word *trinity* means three gods. When a Jew says this word, he usually visualizes an old man with a very long white beard, a baby and a god in the shape of a dove. Some see the trinity as a mother god (Mary), a father god and a baby god, as is common in ancient Middle Eastern religions with similar threesomes.

Interestingly, the word *trinity* appears neither in the New nor the Old Testaments. It is much easier to bring a person to the Lord through the Bible than through church theology. To a Jewish person earnestly enquiring about the deity of Yeshua, I say, "I don't know how many different aspects there are to God. He is much too big for my little finite mind to adequately explain. I do know He can do anything He wants to do and be anything He wants to be. It is a ridiculous mistake for us, the creation, to tell the Creator what He can or cannot do.

"For example, Revelation 3:1 states that there are seven Spirits of God. What does that mean? I do not know, but it simply does not bother me that I do not understand the entirety of the great and mighty God whom I serve." And I explain that anyone who thinks He has God figured out and put in a neat package is a fool.

"What I do know," I continue, "is that I am made in the image of God. I know I have a body. Everybody understands that. I further know I have a soul — the seat of my mind, emotions and will. When I see a corpse, I can readily discern that the body is there, but the soul is not.

"I know about one more area of me because I am a believer. I have a spirit. It is the part of me that is awakened when touched by God. Yeshua referred to the resurrection of a dead spirit into life as being born again." A person who does not have a relationship with God very likely will not know that he has a spirit because his spirit is dead — inactive. Yet the Scriptures speak constantly about man having a spirit.

I believe my nature (body, soul and spirit) somehow reflects God's nature. I have three distinct parts, yet I am unmistakably and irrevocably one person.

God is One. Yeshua stated this in what He said was the most important commandment in the Bible (Mk. 12:29). Yet God's nature has different aspects and manifestations. It is surely His prerogative to reveal Himself in any way He wants, without my approval or permission!

Yeshua said, "I and the Father are one" (Jn. 10:30). I believe that. Yeshua said, "... The Father is greater than I" (Jn. 14:28). I believe that. I believe He is the Word, and the Word is God because the Bible says so (Jn. 1:1). Do I understand it? Absolutely not. I "... see through a glass, darkly ..." (I Cor. 13:12 KJV). But I know Yeshua is my Friend, my Savior and my High Priest because the Bible tells me so. I do not try to theologically dissect God for Jewish people. I think that would be very foolish indeed.

Through little windows of revelation, I do see glimpses of Him here and there. For example, I see God, the great and mighty God of Israel, as a vast sea. He is everywhere, far beyond the beyond. I can stoop down and fill a glass with water from that sea. As I look into the glass, the contents are truly the same as the sea, qualitatively. The same contents that make the sea the sea, are found in that cup. But not all of the water in the vast sea is in the cup.

Yeshua, the Son of God, "... existed in the form of God ..." (Phil. 2:6) and thus is equal to God qualitatively. However, when Yeshua died on the cross, God did not die! I cannot explain it, but this one thing I know: God raised Yeshua from the dead because He lives in my heart. He changed my life and He answers my prayers. He is my High Priest to God, my Father.

Many times these simple illustrations help a Jewish person overcome the abominable image of three gods. To the Jewish person who is sincerely looking for truth, I suggest that He ask the Father, the God of Israel, if He has a son, and if His son is Yeshua. The writer of Proverbs 30:4 did.

> **Who has ascended into heaven and descended? ... Who has established all the ends of the earth? What is His name or His son's name? Surely you know!**

Why Don't Jewish People Understand the Atonement?

One of the greatest blind spots in Rabbinical Judaism is in regard to the blood atonement. Perhaps this lack of understanding came about as Jewish religious leaders over the years attempted to distance themselves from Christian doctrine. But at the time of Yeshua, the Jews certainly understood and practiced blood sacrifice.

Now the temple is no longer available to make sacrificial offerings. After the destruction of the temple in A.D. 70, rabbis looked for an alternative approach to God. They did not have far to look. All false religions teach basically the same thing — we reach God by doing good deeds.

Rabbinical Judaism today teaches that good deeds give us access to God. But Jewish prophets taught that we are all sinners and deserve to die. We can come into the presence of a just God only when the death penalty has been paid.

> **"'For the life of the flesh is in the blood, and I have given it to you on the altar to make atonement for your**

souls; for it is the blood by reason of the life that makes atonement'" (Lev. 17:11).

If there is no atonement, there can be no redemption, no forgiveness of sin, no way to approach and be in the presence of a holy God.

But Rabbinical Judaism now teaches that sacrificing animals was a primitive tradition the early Hebrews picked up from the heathen nations around them. They explain that Moses, knowing that it was very hard to change everything at once, indulged his people by letting them sacrifice animals. But as far as God is concerned, the rabbis' claim, blood sacrifice has no significance.

This blind spot must be challenged and removed. It is one of the strongest Rabbinical Orthodox doctrines that goes against the teaching of the Jewish prophets. Blood atonement can be found in literally every book and section of the Bible. It was the blood of a lamb that kept the firstborn males of Israel from being killed for their sins. The Hebrews had sinned just like the Egyptians and deserved to die. But blood saved them. When Moses ratified the covenant that God had given him to deliver to Israel, the Book of Exodus records:

> **And Moses took half of the blood and put it in basins, and the *other* half ... he sprinkled on the altar. ... Moses took the blood and sprinkled *it* on the people, and said, "Behold, the blood of the covenant, which the LORD has made with you in accordance with all these words"** (Ex. 24:6, 8).

When the Jewish people understand the significance of an animal dying that they might live, they will understand why Yeshua, the Lamb of God, had to die.

What If Yeshua Is Not the Messiah?

If Yeshua is not the Messiah, what will the real Messiah do when he comes to set up His Kingdom? The Scriptures promise there will be peace and righteousness when the Messiah comes. Evil will no longer rule the world.

If the Messiah were to arrive tomorrow, how would he get rid of the thieves, the robbers, the haters, the anti-Semites, the murderers, the criminals, the dope pushers, the dictators, etc.? Obviously he would have to kill them in order to bring peace. And for peace to reign, there could be no brokenhearted men and women whose spouses have left them to commit adultery. Supposedly, he would have to kill the adulterers.

What about the prostitutes, the perverts, the rapists, the distributors of porn? Would he have to execute them, too? And could He allow women to kill their unborn babies? The Bible says, "No longer will there be *in it* an infant *who lives but a few* days ..." (Isa. 65:20). How would the Messiah deal with abortion?

This hypothetical Messiah would have to kill millions of people — all the bad people — in order to have peace on earth. The problem is, every individual does bad things sometime in his lifetime. What would be the cut-off point? When would a person have to pay for his wrongdoings? Would he have to pay with his life?

Perhaps the Messiah will inject all people with a chemical so that they have no will of their own, thus keeping them from doing bad things. Or will there simply be city-sized prisons where millions of criminals would be locked up? That does not sound like a Messianic reign to me!

Yeshua, the true Messiah, **could not** set up His Kingdom the first time He came. He first had to deal with sin and sinners. In fact, Scriptures like Isaiah 53 and Daniel 9:26 clearly proclaim that the Messiah will first die (because of the need for an eternal atonement for sin), in order to give the sinner a chance to escape God's coming judgment.

If Yeshua is not the Messiah, then another Messiah will have to come and fulfill the words of the prophets of Israel. He will have to be rejected by his nation (Isa. 53:3) and be killed (Isa. 53:7, 8).

How Does the Jewish Person Relate to the Life to Come?

The Tanach (Old Testament) does not reveal very much about heaven and hell. Yes, the concept is there. For example, Daniel 12:2 declares that some of Daniel's people will rise from the dead "... to everlasting life, but the others to disgrace *and* everlasting contempt." And there are other passages about the death and resurrection of the evil and the righteous. However, Jewish people have little understanding of life after death.

What seems to be much clearer to Jewish people is the concept of a judgment that is coming on earth to all humanity, the living and the dead, on the day of the Lord. This gives one an opportunity to explain to a Jewish person that everyone is going to be judged — including him. It will be only those who call on the name of the Lord who will be saved.

Indeed, virtually all the prophets speak about the coming judgment:

Behold, the Lord lays the earth waste, devastates it, distorts its surface, and scatters its inhabitants.

The earth is also polluted by its inhabitants, for they transgressed laws, violated statutes, broke the everlasting covenant.

Therefore, a curse devours the earth, and those who live in it are held guilty. Therefore, the inhabitants of the earth are burned, and few men are left (Isa. 24:1, 5, 6).

It is foolish for anyone to wait and continue in his own way, taking the risk that he will have a chance to repent before it is too late. Remember the words God told Ezekiel to speak to his nation:

"Say to them, 'As I live!' declares the Lord God, 'I take no pleasure in the death of the wicked, but rather that the wicked turn from his way and live. Turn back, turn back from your evil ways! Why then will you die, O house of Israel?'" (Ezek. 33:11).

If the one with whom you are sharing believes that he is okay, he must hear the words of the godly prophet Isaiah:

For all of us have become like one who is unclean, and all our righteous deeds [note: not our *bad deeds*] are like a filthy garment; and all of us wither like a leaf, and our iniquities, like the wind, take us away (Isa. 64:6).

So what does one do, and when should he do it? King David said,

**... Today, if you would hear His voice, do not harden
your hearts, as at Meribah, as in the day of Massah in
the wilderness (Psa. 95:7, 8).**

David goes on to explain what happened to the forefathers who would
not repent. God loathed them, and they died in the wilderness.

Moses, the giver of God's covenant, foresaw that the people of Israel
would go astray, fall into sin, and great trouble would come on them
(Deut. 28). This trouble would continue to harass the Jewish nation
until the people repented.

God, knowing all things, foretold that at the time when the Jewish
people return to their own land, God Himself would do a work on their
hearts: His people would finally turn to Him and receive His redemption.

**"And the Lᴏʀᴅ your God will bring you into the land
which your fathers possessed, and you shall possess it ...**

"Moreover the Lᴏʀᴅ your God will circumcise your heart and the heart
of your descendants, to love the Lᴏʀᴅ your God with all your heart and
with all your soul, in order that you may live" (Deut. 30:5, 6).

Every Jew must ask himself: Do I want to live for eternity? Or do I want
to die in my sin? Do I want my children, my family and my friends to
die in their sins and to come under the judgment of God? Do I want to
trust that my good deeds will meet the holy standard of God? Or do I
want to live and help others live also?

If the last question is answered in the affirmative, then one must LOOK
FOR AN ATONEMENT TO COVER THE SINS ALREADY COMMITTED.
Remember what Moses said? It is the blood that makes atonement for
sins.

This is where Yeshua our Messiah provides the answer. He is the Jewish
answer to the great Jewish dilemma. He is the only One Who came to
earth to lay down His life as an atonement for the sins of His people. He
did it just as Isaiah the prophet said He would (Isa. 53).

He is the only person Who claimed to be the Son of God — and proved
it by healing the sick, loving the poor and giving hope to prostitutes

and wicked men. He gave little attention to the self-righteous. He said He came to help sinners. Those who saw themselves as righteous did not realize their need of atonement.

Yeshua is the only person who died for our sins and then rose from the dead; some 500 Jews witnessed the fact (I Cor. 15:6). I say to my Jewish friends, "He will atone for your sins and redeem you, just as God promised you. It is a gift to you. You must only come humbly and accept this gift. Accepting this gift of atonement is admitting that you yourself are not righteous enough to cut it with God. But neither is anybody else."

The Righteous Shall Live By Faith

If a Jew does not want to accept Yeshua's offer of atonement, then the only other possible means for the sinner to make atonement is by sacrificing animals as Israelites did in the Bible times. But the Bible also says that the slaughtered animal must be offered before the tabernacle (later inside the temple) — where the presence of God dwelled. Otherwise, the sacrifice was unacceptable, and the person was cursed by God (Lev. 17:3, 4).

The Good News is that Yeshua fulfilled the Law's requirement. He died for our sins one whole generation (40 years) before the Temple was destroyed. But He, having risen from the grave, offered His sacrifice (His body) for His people in the heavenly Temple — the one Moses copied, the one in which the Lord's presence dwells forever (Ex. 25:40; Heb. 9:11, 12, 24). God has made a way for the sinner!

"So remember, not only did Yeshua die," I tell Jewish people, "but He arose from the dead and returned to His Father. What does that mean to you? It means that He will bring the Spirit of God to come and live in your spirit — His new temple built without hands — giving you new birth, a new lease on life. And the Spirit of God will show you the way to go, to live the life of a Jew redeemed by God Himself. He will then allow you the honor of leading a life planned by Him, guided by Him and protected by Him, just as in the times of the Bible."

Why Was Israel Chosen?

Better put, the question should be: For what *purpose* was Israel chosen? If you ask an Israeli this question, almost certainly he will answer with a smile, perhaps somewhat cynically, somewhat sadly, "We were chosen by God to suffer." The biblical prototype referred to is the righteous Job. Job was a good man, yet he lost everything. So it has been with Israel, the Israeli concludes.

This book is certainly not the place for a study of Job — a complex subject. But it can be said with certainty: God did not choose Israel for the exclusive or primary purpose of suffering. According to the Bible, *God chose Israel to be a light to the nations*.

"Arise, shine; for your light has come, and the glory of the LORD has risen upon you.

"For behold, darkness will cover the earth, and deep darkness the peoples; but the LORD will rise upon you, and His glory will appear upon you.

"And nations will come to your light, and kings to the brightness of your rising" (Isa. 60:1-3).

Even when Israel has not been serving God, *she has still been the model of God's methods of dealing with mankind*. When Israel served God, the Lord made Israel the head and not the tail (Deut. 28:13). On the other hand, if she failed God, she was punished and suffered great evil. Literally hundreds of Scriptures confirm this principle.

In many other ways, Israel is God's living example through which He reveals Himself and His ways. Through His dealings with Israel, the God of all the earth demonstrates how He relates to other peoples and nations. They, too, will be blessed for obeying God — and cursed for going their own way.

Most of all, the nation of Israel was chosen to be God's messenger to the ends of the earth. Many Israelis are aware of this God-given duty and obligation. But they will answer, "The Jews *are* being a light to the nations. With all our brilliant scientists and doctors, we are bringing good into the world." That may be true, but the light to which the Scriptures refer is God and not brilliant scientists.

And He said to Me, "You are My Servant, Israel,

in Whom I will show My glory.

"... I will also make You a light of the nations

so that My salvation may reach to the end of the earth" (Isa. 49:3, 6).

The Scriptures reveal the time of Israel's greatest spiritual productivity will be when she is again rooted and settled in her land. This verse in Isaiah speaks of *spiritual* fruit:

In the days to come Jacob will take root (return to her land and her God), Israel will blossom and sprout; and they will fill the whole world with fruit (Isa. 27:6).

Israel: A Nation of Missionaries

I sometimes have fun with my Israeli friends, telling them that God's plan for the Jews is for them to be missionaries. They of course are dismayed because "missionary" is such a feared and hated word among them. But the Bible spells it out in no uncertain terms:

"'... and you shall be to Me a kingdom of priests and a holy nation.' ..." (Ex. 19:6)

What is a priest but one who ministers to the spiritual needs of others? The Jews are to lead many to God!

"... 'In those days ten men from all the nations will grasp the garment of a Jew saying, "Let us go with you, for we have heard that God is with you"'" (Zech. 8:23).

The prophets proclaim this over and over again. Look at some of the Scriptures.

"And the surviving remnant of the house of Judah shall again take root downward and bear fruit upward. ..." (Isa. 37:31)

But you will be called the priests of the Lord;

... You will be spoken of *as* ministers of our God. ...

(Isa.61:6)

And in that day you will say, "... Make known His deeds among the peoples ..."

... Let this be known throughout the earth (Isa. 12:4, 5).

And what about this passage?

"... As soon as Zion travailed, she also brought forth her sons. ...

"And I will set a sign among them and will send survivors from them to the nations: Tarshish, Put, Lud, Meshech, Rosh, Tubal, and Javan, to the distant coastlands that have neither heard My fame nor seen My glory. And they will declare My glory among the nations" (Isa. 66:8, 19).

And here's a Scripture that has been used literally thousands of times by Gentiles, without realizing the passage is primarily addressed to Israel!

So rejoice, O sons of Zion, and be glad in the LORD your God ...

"Thus you will know that I am in the midst of Israel ...

"And it will come about after this that I will pour out My Spirit on all mankind; and your sons and daughters will prophesy, your old men will dream dreams,

"your young men will see visions.

"And even on the male and female servants I will pour out My Spirit in those days ..." (Joel 2:23, 27-29).

One should not, of course, limit these prophetic promises to the Jewish people. What God does for His model, Israel, He will do for others if they follow Him. However, we cannot ignore that, in these verses, Joel is speaking to the Jewish people first! And other prophets back these promises with their own declarations.

"Sing for joy and be glad, O daughter of Zion; for behold I am coming and I will dwell in your midst,"

declares the LORD.

"And many nations will join themselves to the LORD in that day and will become My people. ..." (Zech. 2:10, 11).

In that day the Branch of the LORD will be beautiful and glorious, and the fruit of the earth *will* be the pride and the adornment of the survivors of Israel (Isa. 4:2).

Although Israel is not yet fulfilling these Scriptures, she is still serving God's purposes. Though most Jewish people are returning to Israel in unbelief, the nation's physical resurrection nonetheless declares the faithfulness of God. He is keeping His promise to be a God to the children of Abraham.

God has been long-suffering with the children of Israel and will surely bring them back into salvation. In the same manner, He is illustrating that He will bring back the backslidden sons and daughters of believing parents who have sought the Lord on their children's behalf. In other words, Israel is a model through which He reveals His principles of mercy, judgment, faithfulness and righteousness.

How Can I Believe in a God Who Would Allow the Holocaust to Happen?

In Israel and in the rest of the world, there is a whole generation of atheistic Jews who were born to Orthodox parents. These Jews are the Ashkenazi (European) Jews who went through the Holocaust. Their parents and relatives were traditionally religious (as the Jewish community had been for centuries).

Although some Western European Jews in the early 20th century had become "modern" and left religion behind, most Jews — especially those in Eastern Europe and Russia — were very Orthodox. They followed the religion of their fathers as it had been practiced for centuries. Six million Jews, most of whom were religious, were destroyed by Hitler. Consequently, the vast majority of survivors became atheists — a few might prefer the term agnostic. Their reasoning: If a God such as described in the Bible exists, He would never have let the Holocaust occur. If this God chose Israel as His own peculiar treasure, how could He have allowed a disaster of such unimaginable proportions to happen? Their conclusion: There is no God.

To make matters worse, the Nazis — professing Catholics and Protestants — were the killers who carried out the atrocities.

The Jews conclude that Yeshua could never be the Messiah, since He was the head of a religion whose people massacred the people of the book. Some of them reason that God can't have a son if He Himself doesn't exist. In their eyes, Yeshua has proved He is a false Messiah because of what His followers have done to the Jews for the last 1,900 years.

The Scriptures clearly teach that the people of Israel are God's chosen people. Why, then, did He allow the Holocaust to occur?

> **"For you are a holy people to the LORD your God; the LORD your God has chosen you to be a people for His own possession out of all the peoples who are on the face of the earth" (Deut. 7:6).**

How then could God allow a third of Israel to be exterminated? The answer lies in understanding the *requirements* and *conditions* of the covenants God made with Israel.

The covenant God made with Abraham and his seed promises that God will be a God to the children of Abraham forever. And that He will prosper and bless this nation and give Israel her own land (Gen. 12:1-3, 15:18 and 17:7). Except for the ordinance of circumcision, this is an unconditional covenant. In other words, the only requirement for a natural son of Abraham (a physical Jew) to be a beneficiary of this covenant is circumcision (Gen. 17:10-14). It is because of this everlasting covenant with Abraham, Isaac and Jacob (Israel) that the Jewish people exist today (Psa. 105:8-11). This covenant can never be annulled (Gal. 3:17).

But some 400 years after God made the covenant with Abraham, He made a second covenant with Israel through His servant Moses. This covenant, unlike the Abrahamic covenant, was very conditional. The conditions are found in Deuteronomy 28.

"Now it shall be, if you will diligently obey the Lord your God, being careful to do all His commandments which I command you today, the Lord your God will set you high above all the nations of the earth.

"And all these blessings shall come upon you and overtake you, if you will obey the Lord your God" (Deut. 28:1, 2).

In summary, *if* Israel would obey the commands of God given through Moses, she would be the greatest of all nations and superabundantly blessed by God.

However, there was a second condition to the Law of Moses:

"But it shall come about, if you will not obey the Lord your God, to observe to do all His commandments and His statutes with which I charge you today, that all these curses shall come upon you and overtake you ..." **(Deut. 28:15).**

The rest of this chapter details the kind of curses that will come upon Israel if she does not keep the Mosaic Covenant.

"... then the Lord will bring extraordinary plagues on you and your descendants, even severe and lasting plagues, and miserable and chronic sicknesses. ...

"And it shall come about that as the Lord delighted over you to prosper you, and multiply you, so the Lord will delight over you to make you perish and destroy you; and you shall be torn from the land where you are entering to possess it.

"Moreover, the Lord will scatter you among all peoples, from one end of the earth to the other end of the earth; and there you shall serve other gods, wood and stone, which you or your fathers have not known.

"And among those nations you shall find no rest, and there shall be no resting place for the sole of your foot; but there the Lord will give you a trembling heart, failing of eyes, and despair of soul.

"So your life shall hang in doubt before you; and you shall be in dread night and day, and shall have no assurance of your life" (Deut. 28:59, 63-66).

These verses, then, explain the history of Israel for the last 2,500 years. Israel has seen two dispersions, the destruction of her Temple twice, and genocide to her people in many countries — the worst disaster being the destruction wreaked by the Nazis, whose ultimate plan involved taking over the world and exterminating every Jew on the planet.

The majority of the Jews who died in the Holocaust were pious and observant of the Law. However, regardless of how pious and observant a person is, every one of us has broken God's Torah. Many Scripture passages witness to that. King David said,

> **The Lord has looked down from heaven upon the sons of men, to see if there are any who understand, who seek after God.**

They have all turned aside; together they have become corrupt; there is **no one** who does good, not even one (Psa. 14:2, 3).

We repeat the words of Isaiah:

> **For all of us have become like one who is unclean, and all our righteous deeds are like a filthy garment (Isa. 64:6).**

All of us like sheep have gone astray, each of us has turned to his own way ... (Isa. 53:6).

Even with the explicit language of Moses and the prophets, however, the religious leaders of Israel have not seen the association between the suffering of Israel and her breaking the Torah (Law of Moses).

> **"So all these curses shall come on you and pursue you and overtake you until you are destroyed, because you would not obey the Lord your God by keeping His commandments and His statutes which He commanded you ..." (Deut. 28:45).**

When Daniel the prophet asked God to return His people to the land of their fathers, he acknowledged that they were scattered and suffering because they transgressed the Torah.

> **So I gave my attention to the Lord God to seek *Him by* prayer and supplications, with fasting, sackcloth and ashes.**

And I prayed to the Lord my God and confessed and said, "Alas, O Lord, the great and awesome God, who keeps His covenant and lovingkindness for those who love Him and keep His commandments,

"we have sinned, committed iniquity, acted wickedly, and rebelled, even turning aside from Thy commandments and ordinances.

"... nor have we obeyed the voice of the Lord our God, to walk in His teachings which He set before us through His servants the prophets.

"Indeed all Israel has transgressed Thy law and turned aside, not obeying Thy voice; so the curse has been poured out on us, along with the oath which is written in the law of Moses the servant of God, for we have sinned against Him. ...

"As it is written in the law of Moses, all this calamity has come on us; yet we have not sought the favor of the Lord our God by turning from our iniquity and giving attention to Thy truth. ..." (Dan. 9:3-5, 10, 11, 13)

Indeed Daniel was a righteous man; but he, too, had to confess his sins. If all Israel transgressed the Torah, why then did God not let Israel be completely destroyed? In the New Testament, Paul explained why Israel still exists:

> **... the Law, which came four hundred and thirty years later, does not invalidate a covenant previously ratified by God, so as to nullify the promise.**

For if the inheritance is based on law, it is no longer based on a promise; but God has granted it to Abraham by means of a promise (Gal. 3:17, 18).

It is because of the promise God gave Abraham that Israel is still here and will yet fulfill God's plan for her as His chosen people. This is explained by Ezekiel. He says that first Israel will be punished for breaking the (Mosaic) covenant.

> **For thus says the Lord GOD, "I will also do with you as you have done, you who have despised the oath by breaking the covenant ..." (Ezek. 16:59).**

But Ezekiel reveals that because of the earlier Abrahamic covenant, God will establish yet a third covenant.

> **"Nevertheless, I will remember My covenant with you in the days of your youth, and I will establish an everlasting covenant with you. ..." (Ezek. 16:60)**

Logically, this new covenant would have to provide for Israel's release from the curses of the Mosaic covenant in order that the promises of the Abrahamic covenant may be fully implemented.

How is a Jew Released from the Curse of the Law?

A Jew who is truly seeking God will naturally ask, "What does a Jew do to be freed from the curse of the Law?" Jeremiah gives the answer. Even though the types of sin committed by Israel — and all mankind — may vary from century to century, God's principles toward sin and repentance remain unchanged.

> **"... 'Return, faithless Israel,' declares the LORD; 'I will not look upon you in anger. For I am gracious,' declares the Lord; 'I will not be angry forever.**

'Only acknowledge your iniquity ...

'And I will bring you to Zion'" (Jer. 3:12-14).

Even Daniel, a righteous prophet, acknowledged his sin and then prayed for forgiveness:

> **"O Lord, hear! O Lord, forgive! O Lord, listen and take action! For Thine own sake, O my God, do not delay, because Thy city and Thy people are called by Thy**

name" (Dan. 9:19).

If You Don't Like Numbers, Skip This Section!

While Daniel was praying, an angel appeared to him to explain how Israel would be brought back to God. The passage is difficult to understand. The time units used by the angel to reveal when these things would happen are obscure. Yet one thing is very clear: The angel is speaking of God's forgiveness of Israel's sins and the appearance of the Messiah.

> **Now while I [Daniel] was speaking and praying, and confessing my sin and the sin of my people Israel, and presenting my supplication ...**

[the angel Gabriel] gave *me* instruction ... and said, "O Daniel, I have now come forth to give you insight with understanding. ...

"Seventy weeks [better translated from Hebrew as seventy sets of seven] have been decreed for your people and your holy city ..." (Dan. 9:20, 22, 24).

The angel then proceeded to tell him that within this time God would 1) finish transgression; 2) make an end of sin; 3) make atonement for iniquity; and 4) bring in everlasting righteousness (Dan. 9:24).

Anyone can see that the angelic time unit of seventy sets of seven has not yet passed because everlasting righteousness has not yet come to the earth. But the angel also told Daniel:

> **"So you are to know and discern *that* from the issuing of a decree to restore and rebuild Jerusalem until Messiah the Prince *there will be* seven weeks and sixty-two weeks ..."** (Dan. 9:25).

The angel was saying that, from the issue of the order to rebuild Jerusalem until the Messiah's coming, a time of 69 sets of seven would intervene. But the angel also adds that this Messiah "... will be cut off and have nothing ..." (Dan 9:26). Are we saying that Daniel prophesied that the Messiah would come and be killed? Most certainly.

We who believe that the Messiah is Yeshua must conclude that the 69 sets of seven have already passed. Thus, one more set of seven remains before the Messianic reign begins.

If a set of seven represents seven years, then 69 sets of seven is equivalent to 483 years. According to this passage, God's special clock started when the command to rebuild Jerusalem was issued.

Scholars differ in their calculations and no one knows exactly when Artaxerxes made his decree to rebuild Jerusalem when the Jews returned from Babylon. It was most likely sometime in the middle of the fifth century B.C. If 69 x 7 (483) years is added, the resulting date falls in the era when Yeshua lived and died. No other person fulfilled Daniel's prophecy during that era. Only Yeshua, Son of David, proclaimed His Messiahship and then foretold his death.

What is the importance of this? Daniel came in sackcloth and ashes and confessed his sin. And God (through His angel) showed Daniel how, and even when, atonement would be made — by the killing of the Messiah! By His sacrifice, the Messiah releases every Jew who believes in Him from the transgression and resulting curse of the Torah.

The great prophet Isaiah described how the Messiah of Israel was to be made a sacrifice for the sins of Israel.

> **But he was wounded and bruised for *our* sins. He was beaten that we might have peace; He was lashed — and we were healed!**

We — every one of us — have strayed away like sheep! *We*, who left God's paths to follow our own. Yet God laid on *him* the guilt and sins of every one of us! ...

From prison and trial they led him away to his death. But who among the people of that day realized it was their sins that he was dying for — that he was suffering their punishment?

> **... my righteous Servant shall make many to be counted righteous before God, for he shall bear all their sins.**

> **... because he has poured out his soul unto death. He**

was counted as a sinner ... (Isa. 53:5-6, 8, 11-12, LB).

We must tell Jewish people that when our sins are covered and we are no longer guilty as Law breakers, God Himself will write His Torah in our hearts. He will not only be our God, but this time we will be His people!

"Behold, days are coming," declares the LORD, "when I will make a new covenant with the house of Israel and with the house of Judah,

not like the covenant which I made with their fathers in the day I took them by the hand to bring them out of the land of Egypt, My covenant which they broke, although I was a husband to them," declares the LORD.

"But this is the covenant which I will make with the house of Israel after those days," declares the LORD, "I will put my law within them, and on their heart I will write it; and I will be their God, and they shall be My people" (Jer. 31:31-33).

Paul explains to us that under the new covenant we no longer have to earn our righteousness by perfectly keeping the Law.

Messiah redeemed us from the curse of the Law, having become a curse for us ... (Gal. 3:13).

With the Spirit of God writing His Law in our hearts, we are now released from the demands of the Mosaic Law and from its curses when we break it.

Are we then lawless, free to live in spiritual anarchy? God forbid! We now "... serve in newness of the Spirit and not in oldness of the letter" (Rom. 7:6). "... for the letter kills [how well we know that!], but the Spirit gives life" (II Cor. 3:6).

Didn't Yeshua Teach Jews They Should Eat Pig?

Through our years of sharing Scriptural truths with Jewish people, we have found one notion planted almost universally in the Jewish mind: the New Testament can't be the Word of God and Yeshua can't be the Messiah because the New Testament and Yeshua taught that Jews should eat pig.

I categorically deny that the New Testament teaches such a doctrine, and we will go through the Scriptures to prove this point.

First, let us examine what the Old Testament says. Under the Law of Moses, Israel was to eat types of animals that were clean unto God and could also be used as sacrifices. Those animals had to chew the cud and have split hooves. Oxen (the cow, bull, heifer), sheep, goats and various deer (moose, antelope, gazelle, etc.) were appointed by God as food.

These animals, through their double stomachs, were able to separate and prevent most disease-ridden substances from entering the flesh. But a pig, which does not chew the cud, literally becomes what he eats. This is why pork can be dangerous for humans to consume and why the growth, feeding and marketing of pigs must be carefully supervised.

The animal with a split hoof is protected from disease-causing substances which otherwise might enter through his feet. An animal without a split hoof has less protection from impurities on the ground. For example, a lion — which has no split hooves — can become infected with parasites through his paws.

The same principles apply to certain scavenging birds and to fish that do not have both fins and scales. One such fish is the catfish — a popular food, but a born scavenger! Shrimp and lobsters are also scavengers.

Creeping things — such as rats, snakes, roaches and other bugs (except locusts and grasshoppers) — were forbidden to Jewish people. (See Deuteronomy 14 and Leviticus 11.)

It is interesting to note that the animals God permitted Israel to eat are not instinctive killers. They do not eat the flesh of other animals.

The animals approved by God for human consumption are thus the same ones Israel was to offer as atoning sacrifices for sins. Indeed, when we kill an animal to eat, we are taking its life so that we may live (through eating). In this sense, killing an animal for food is a type of substitute sacrifice.

We have pointed out that, in many different ways, Israel is God's model through which he dramatizes His principles and truths.

We could illustrate this repeatedly through the Old and New Testament Scriptures. For example, every time a Jew eats an animal with a split hoof and a divided stomach, he is testifying of God's commandment that we divide the unclean and the filth of this world from the clean.

Furthermore, Jews have been instructed by God not to eat the blood of an animal. Under the Law of Moses, the Jew who partakes of the blood is cut off from the people of Israel. The blood represents the soul of the animal, and the soul (blood) is the substitute atonement that God provided to take away the sins of a human being (Lev. 17:10-14).

This law was later passed on to be observed by Gentiles (Acts 15:19-20). So when Jew or Gentile does not eat the blood of an animal, he is illustrating on the earth-stage that the blood belongs to God. It is precious to Him, because He gave it to us as an atonement for our sins.

What Does the New Testament Say About Kashrut (Eating Only Clean Animals)?

Does Yeshua or Paul instruct Jews to eat unkosher animals? Certainly not! Surprised? Let us look at the Scriptures.

Most Israeli schoolchildren were taught (mistaught) the story found in Acts 10. The typical non-believing Jew will tell you that Peter received a vision from God telling him to eat pork and shrimp! According to the Bible, Peter received a vision from God in which a sheet full of "... four-footed animals and crawling creatures of the earth and birds of the air" descended from the sky (Acts 10:12).

Some people envision this scene as a sheet coming down containing barbecued pork chops and lobster cooked in butter, with a side of fried shrimp and fresh crabs. Actually, the vision was a sheet filled with rats, cats, snakes, spiders, roaches, bats and every other unclean and undesirable living thing. As the story continues, we do not find a Peter who was anxious to sit down to this heavenly "banquet." Rather, Peter "... was greatly perplexed in mind as to what the vision which he had seen might be ..." (Acts 10:17). Peter testified during this vision that he had never eaten unkosher or unclean food in his entire life.

While Peter was meditating on the meaning of the vision, a knock came at his door. The visitors had been sent to deliver a message: Peter was invited to a Gentile's home. This had never happened to him before. But it was at the house of Cornelius that Peter received the understanding of the vision.

> **And he said to them, "You yourselves know how unlawful it is for a man who is a Jew to associate with a foreigner or to visit him; and *yet* God has shown me that I should not call any man unholy or unclean. ...**
>
> **"but in every nation the man who fears Him and does what is right, is welcome to Him" (Acts 10:28, 35).**

In summary, God told Peter that He had made a way for *all* men — both Jew and Gentile — to approach the throne of grace, a way which bypassed the cleanliness laws relating to the earthly temple. The vision had nothing to do with advocating the eating of unkosher food.

When I explained the meaning of this vision to an archeology professor at the Hebrew University, he responded, "Oh, that's a good interpretation of this passage!" I told him, "That's no interpretation. Those are direct quotes from the mouth of Peter." In short, there is not a single implication in this passage that Peter was to start eating pork chops.

A Jew avoided ceremonial uncleanness because under the Law of Moses, it prevented him from entering the temple — in which was the presence of God. The Gentiles, who did not follow the Scriptures to maintain ceremonial cleanliness could never enter the temple. For instance, at the time of her monthly period, a Jewish woman could not enter the temple. Other things which made a person ceremonially unclean included contact with the dead, leprosy, sexual discharge, and child birth. Anyone unclean who did enter in was cut off from the community of Israel, excommunicated by God and expelled from His presence in the temple — a fate worse than death.

> **"'But the man who is unclean and does not purify himself from uncleanness, that person shall be cut off from the midst of the assembly, because he has defiled**

> **the sanctuary of the LORD; the water for impurity has not been sprinkled on him, he is unclean. ...'" (Num. 19:20)**

Thus the religious rulers were willing to kill Yeshua, but they were not willing to become ceremonially unclean to do it — so great was the fear of being excommunicated by God.

> **They led Jesus therefore from Caiaphas into the Praetorium, and it was early; and they themselves did not enter into the Praetorium in order that they might not be defiled, but might eat the Passover (Jn. 18:28).**

The Passover lamb had to be slaughtered in the temple and one had to be clean to fulfill this commandment. Furthermore, the Bible declares that one could not even eat the Passover lamb at the appointed time if he was ceremonially unclean (Num. 9:10-13).

Through Peter's vision, God was signaling to the Jews that Yeshua's blood ratified the new covenant, which the prophets claimed would have a different set of conditions (Jer. 31:31-33). When Yeshua died, the veil of the temple was supernaturally torn in two (Matt. 27:51). The middle wall of partition which had kept unclean people out, was no longer needed; the temple in which God lives would now be His people. Men and women of all nations are now welcome into God's presence. Gentiles are no longer considered unclean outsiders as they were under the Mosaic covenant.

If Israel today were still dependent on the Law of Moses for ritual cleanliness before God, then all of Israel today is unclean. There is no biblical basis for a Jew to be ceremonially cleansed from his uncleanness without a functioning temple.

But let us return to the subject of kashrut. Did Yeshua not tell the Jews to eat unkosher (profane) foods?

> **And the Pharisees and some of the scribes gathered together around Him when they had come from Jerusalem,**
>
> **and had seen that some of His disciples were eating their bread with impure hands, that is, unwashed.**

(For the Pharisees and all the Jews do not eat unless they carefully wash their hands, *thus* observing the traditions of the elders;

and *when they come* from the market place, they do not eat unless they cleanse themselves; and there are many other things which they have received in order to observe, such as the washing of cups and pitchers and copper pots.) (Mk. 7:1-4).

The one (and only) subject discussed in this passage here is the washing of hands and vessels called in Hebrew *n'tilat yadayim.* This ceremonial procedure, ordained by oral or Rabbinical Law, is not mandated by the Bible. Note the religious leaders' question:

And the Pharisees and the scribes asked Him, "Why do Your disciples not walk according to the tradition of the elders, but eat their bread with impure hands?" (Mk. 7:5)

As we see, the question troubling the Pharisees and scribes was not, "Why are your disciples eating pork or shrimp?" but "Why are they eating without ceremonially washing their hands?"

If someone had even unknowingly touched something dead — a leprous person, bodily wastes, etc. — he was unclean. Everything he or she touched became unclean. Therefore, reasoned the rabbis, food became unclean also. The purpose of washing one's hands before eating was to make oneself ritually clean. However, it was not the Scriptural method.

The Torah explained how to get rid of uncleanness (Lev. 12-15). It also gave Israel Yom Kippur (Day of Atonement) to atone for, among other sins, any unknown uncleanness (Lev. 16). But through oral law, the rabbis added many extra precautions and rituals. The oral law carried the same weight, so the rabbis said, as the written Word of God.

Yeshua answered that these rabbinical leaders were breaking the Law of Moses, but keeping their own man-made traditions. He actually accused them of "... invalidating the word of God by your tradition which you have handed down; and you do many such things like that"

(Mk. 7:13).

Yeshua then explained to the crowd that foods touched by an unclean thing are not ritually unclean. Food doesn't defile the heart. The important issue is what proceeds from a man's heart, for that is what defiles a man. He was pointing his listeners to the major problem of mankind — an unclean heart. What good is it for a man to eat ritually clean food when his heart is filthy?

He then "declared all foods clean" (Mk. 7:19). Bear in mind the subject of this conversation: ceremonial hand washing before eating. Yeshua was clearly declaring that a food's ritual cleanliness was not affected by hand washing. Note He did not say all animals are clean, and thus fit for food. He was not commanding His Jewish disciples to eat snakes, rats, lizards and pigs, *which were not considered food by the nation of Israel*.

If Yeshua had advocated eating profane animals, the rabbinical Jews surely would have immediately rioted in the streets of Jerusalem. But never at any time — not even at his trial, when the leaders were looking for accusations — was Yeshua accused of persuading His disciples to eat unkosher animals.

Some 20 years later, Peter received the vision of the sheet. Recall that he claimed never to have eaten an unclean or unholy thing (animal) in his entire lifetime, although he *had* eaten with ceremonially unclean hands. So he, too, had certainly understood that Yeshua was speaking of ceremonial uncleanness concerning foods.

Should Gentiles Keep Kashrut?

In another very enlightening passage in Acts, the Jerusalem council debated whether the Gentiles should keep the Torah (Acts 15). It seems many Christians suppose Peter and James to have said, "Listen brethren! We Jews who follow Yeshua don't keep the Torah. Since we eat unkosher animals, etc., why are we even discussing whether the Gentiles should keep the Law?"

But that is not what these two apostles said. Instead, they declared that no Jew had been able to bear the yoke of keeping the Torah perfectly.

"But we believe that we are saved through the grace of the Lord Jesus, in the same way as they also are. ...

"Therefore it is my judgment that we do not trouble those who are turning to God from among the Gentiles ...

"For it seemed good to the Holy Spirit and to us to lay upon you no greater burden than these essentials:

"that you abstain from things sacrificed to idols and from blood and from things strangled and from fornication; if you keep yourselves free from such things, you will do well. ..." (Acts 15:11, 19, 28, 29).

And so these apostles did not demand of the Gentiles to keep the kosher laws. They did state that the Law of Moses is preached every Saturday in the synagogues — indicating that if a Gentile wants to learn of the Torah, he is free to go there (Acts 15:21). But since it had nothing to do with salvation, either for Jew or Gentile, there was no point in asking Gentiles to keep a Jewish life-style.

We emphasize, however, that the Jewish apostles would have approached this issue in a completely different manner if they themselves had not been living according to the Torah. A vast difference exists between obedience to God's Law because we are saved by grace and obedience in an attempt to earn our righteousness and entrance to God's presence. We keep the commandment, "You shall not kill" as a *result* of our love of God, not in an attempt to earn God's favor.

This important subject deserves a complete book to adequately consider the issue. (For further reading, see David Stern's book, *The Jewish Manifesto*, available from Jewish New Testament Publications, P.O. Box 1313, Clarksville, Maryland 21029, USA.)

But someone might say, did not Paul advocate eating unkosher foods? What about Galatians 2 when Paul condemns Peter for not eating with the Gentiles? Again, this case dealt not with unkosher animals, but with ceremonial uncleanness.

Here is the same Peter who had been given the heavenly vision which specifically told him not to count anyone unclean whom God declared clean. And then Peter has the audacity to go against this revelation that God had personally given to him. He refused to eat with "unclean" Gentiles, because he could not do so and remain ceremonially clean.

Paul reminds Peter that he is "unclean" (as far as Jewish tradition is concerned), because he never strictly kept the hand washing traditions anyway. Remember Peter was one of those disciples mentioned in Matthew 15 who ate with unwashed, unclean hands. So why was he suddenly worried about becoming ceremonially unclean by eating with Gentiles?

Besides the fact that we are saved by grace and not by works, I believe there is another reason that the Lord declared all foods ceremonially clean. Israel could not be a light to the nations and preach the Good News if Jews could not eat and fellowship with Gentiles. It would have been a terrible block to Israel's commission to reach the world for God.

But what about I Corinthians 10:27, in which Paul says a person should eat anything given to him? In this passage, Paul is dealing with the subject of food offered to idols. *He is also writing to the church at Corinth, a group of Gentile believers.* Let us recall the Jerusalem Council decision in Acts 15 concerning Gentiles' relationship to Jewish Law:

1. The apostles would not burden the Gentiles with keeping the Jewish Law as such.

2. They did ask them not to eat food contaminated by idols, not to commit fornication, to abstain from what has been strangled and from consuming blood.

In I Corinthians 8:4, Paul explains that there actually is no such thing as an idol. It is nothing in God's sight. So if a believer who loves God accidentally or unknowingly eats foods offered to idols, there is no intrinsic evil in the food that will bring sin into his life. With God, therefore, it doesn't matter if we eat or do not eat. However, Paul says, our duty is to be a help and not a stumbling block to our fellow brethren. We must beware what foods we eat, so as to in no way hinder another's spiritual life.

These remarks Paul made to the Gentiles. He made it clear many times that he was sent by God to bring the Gospel to the Gentiles: "... I had been entrusted with the gospel to the uncircumcised, just as Peter had been to the circumcised" (Gal. 2:7). Probably for that reason he did not touch on the subject of unkosher animals here at all.

Paul does seem to be speaking about unkosher food in Romans 14, although we cannot be absolutely certain. But let us presume that he is.

Let us always keep in mind that he is the apostle to the Gentiles. Most of his teaching is directed to them. Thus he would have taught in line with the decision of the Jerusalem Council.

However, the context in which he seemingly speaks of kashrut is in connection with *judging others*. What if someone keeps the Sabbath? What if he does not? What if someone's a vegetarian? What if another eats everything, whatever that might be?

Paul's answer: It's none of your business (Rom. 14:10-13). If we are mature, we will not judge another brother on these outward habits. Since we are all saved by grace, each man will be judged by God, not by us.

Then Paul goes on to explain to his Gentile disciples that he believed no animal (be it a spider or moth) is intrinsically unclean before God. Therefore, our salvation is not at stake. Our relationship with God is not at stake. Since the middle wall of partition has been broken down, we do not have to worry about being ceremonially clean. God dwells inside of us! So let a brother's obedience to God be between him and the Lord.

On the other hand, whether we are Jew or Gentile we are to eat nothing that would be offensive or an obstacle to our brother.

> **Let not him who eats regard with contempt him who does not eat, and let not him who does not eat judge him who eats, for God has accepted him.**

> **Who are you to judge the servant of another? To his own master he stands or falls; and stand he will, for the Lord is able to make him stand.**

> One man regards one day above another, another
> regards every day *alike*. Let each man be fully convinced
> in his own mind.
>
> He who observes the day, observes it for the Lord, and
> he who eats, does so for the Lord, for he gives thanks to
> God; and he who eats not, for the Lord he does not eat,
> and gives thanks to God. ...
>
> But you, why do you judge your brother? Or you again,
> why do you regard your brother with contempt? For we
> shall all stand before the judgment seat of God. ...
>
> So then each one of us shall give account of himself to
> God.
>
> Therefore let us not judge one another any more, but
> rather determine this — not to put an obstacle or
> stumbling block in a brother's way. ...
>
> Do not tear down the work of God for the sake of food.
> All things indeed are clean, but they are evil for the man
> who eats and gives offense.
>
> It is good not to eat meat or to drink wine, or *to do
> anything* by which your brother stumbles (Rom. 14:3-6,
> 10, 12, 13, 20, 21).

Paul exhorts thus:

> For he who in this *way* serves Messiah is acceptable to
> God and approved by men (Rom. 14:18).

Paul the Jew Kept Kashrut

It appears that Paul himself rigorously applied this principle to his own
life. He himself testifies numerous times that *he did not break the
Jewish law*. Although he may have taught that no animal is intrinsically
unclean under the new covenant, he himself did not touch unkosher
food! How do we know?

The Book of Acts tells of Paul's last journey to Jerusalem in obedience to God. The apostles heard that he had come. They met with him and listened to him tell of the great salvation of God to the Gentiles. They rejoiced with him.

And when they heard it they *began* glorifying God; and they said to him, "You see, brother, how many thousands there are among the Jews of those who have believed, and they are all zealous for the Law;

and they have been told about you, that you are teaching all the Jews who are among the Gentiles to forsake Moses, telling them not to circumcise their children nor to walk according to the customs" (Acts 21:20, 21).

The leaders of the body of Messiah in Jerusalem then offered this proposal, which we paraphrase: "Paul, we know that this accusation against you is not true. But people have been hearing that you tell the Jews to break the Law (probably in reference to passages like Rom. 14 and Col. 2:16). But to prove that this is *not true*, and that *you never taught Jews to break the Mosaic Law*, we want you to help these four born-again Jewish brethren of ours to complete the Nazarite vow that they have made according to the law of Moses. Pay their expenses and go with them."

"... and all will know that there is nothing to the things which they have been told about you, but that you yourself also walk orderly, keeping the Law" (Acts 21:24).

What a statement! The apostles were telling Paul to prove to everybody that he is a keeper of the Torah (including kosher laws). Some might say, "Well, that's what the apostles *thought*. But that's not what Paul really did."

However, Paul was never wishy-washy in his walk with God. He never would have deceived the apostles into thinking he did something he really had not done. Besides, Paul then proceeded to carefully follow the instructions of the apostles in order to prove that he did "walk orderly, keeping the Law."

Others might say that Paul made a mistake by going to the temple. His attempt to prove himself ended in his arrest and ultimately, in his being sent to Rome. Whether he made a mistake is debatable. I do not believe he did, because God told him that he was going to Rome.

But whether or not he made a mistake has nothing to do with the point we are making here: *The apostles did not believe Paul was telling Jews to break the Torah. They believed that Paul, a Jew, did not break the law. Paul then attempted to prove that these two assumptions were true.*

Earlier in Acts, he himself had made and kept a similar Nazarite vow. "In Cenchrea he had his hair cut, for he was keeping a vow" (Acts 18:18). He strove to get to Jerusalem in order to celebrate the Jewish holiday of Shavuot (Acts 20:16). Moreover, Paul testified from his own mouth that he was a Jew who kept the law!

> **"But this I admit to you, that according to the Way which they call a sect I do serve the God of our fathers, believing everything that is in accordance with the Law, and that is written in the Prophets ..." (Acts 24:14).**

While Paul said in his own defense, "I have committed no offense either against the Law of the Jews or against the temple or against Caesar" (Acts 25:8).

> **And it happened that after three days he called together those who were the leading men of the Jews, and when they had come together, he *began* saying to them, "Brethren, though I had done nothing against our people, or the customs of our fathers, yet I was delivered prisoner from Jerusalem into the hands of the Romans" (Acts 28:17).**

By Paul's own witness, then, we have the "final word" of testimony as to the type of life-style Paul the Jew lived. Committing no offense against the "customs of our fathers" or the law of the Jew, which would most certainly have included keeping the kosher laws, even though he was called to preach the Gospel to the Gentiles.

From this study, we can conclude that absolutely no Scripture in the

New Testament commands Jews to eat unclean animals. What a pity that this misinterpretation of the New Testament may have kept some Jews from seeking salvation through the Messiah, the King of the Jews.

Why is the New Testament Considered Anti-Semitic?

Many, if not a majority of Jewish people, believe the New Testament to be anti-Semitic.

Jewish scholars teach that some New Testament verses show hatred towards Jews and accuse them of deicide — the killing of God.

Though previously we have dealt with the question of who killed Yeshua, we now want to deal directly with the question of anti-Semitism in the New Testament itself. The question arises over Scriptures such as these when Peter preached on the Holiday of Shavuot in Jerusalem:

> **"... this *Man*, delivered up by the predetermined plan and foreknowledge of God, you nailed to a cross by the hands of godless men and put *Him* to death. ..." (Acts 2:23)**

"The God of Abraham, Isaac, and Jacob, the God of our fathers, has glorified His servant Jesus, *the one* whom you delivered up, and disowned in the presence of Pilate, when he had decided to release Him.

"But you disowned the Holy and Righteous One, and asked for a murderer to be granted to you,

"but put to death the Prince of life, *the one* whom God raised from the dead, *a fact* to which we are witnesses. ..." (Acts 3:13-15)

The answer to these accusations is not difficult at all. Firstly, fact is fact and truth is truth.

The Jewish people physically delivered one of their brethren (Yeshua) to the Romans and asked for his death. No one can argue with this fact of history. When the apostles spoke these words to fellow Jews, no one accused them of being anti-Semitic, any more than today a Jewish citizen witnessing in court of a crime he saw another Jew commit would be considered anti-Semitic.

If others later used these Scriptures against the Jewish people, it cannot be blamed on the disciples who witnessed the crucifixion themselves.

The Old Testament relates in detail the rejection of Joseph by his brothers, the sons of Israel. But that does not make the Old Testament anti-Semitic. Indeed, Joseph explained that God was in control all the time. "And as for you, you meant evil against me, *but* God meant it for good ..." (Gen. 50:20). And through the sinful acts of the sons of Israel, Joseph became a type of the Savior of both Israel and the Gentiles.

However, if one *wants* to be anti-Semitic, he really has no need to look to the New Testament. The Old Testament has hundreds of verses much harsher against Israel than New Testament portions. Here are the words of Moses:

> **"For I know that after my death you will act corruptly and turn from the way which I have commanded you; and evil will befall you in the latter days, for you will do that which is evil in the sight of the LORD, provoking Him to anger with the work of your hands" (Deut. 31:29).**

"So all these curses shall come on you and pursue you and overtake you until you are destroyed, because you would not obey the LORD your God by keeping His commandments and His statutes which He commanded you.

"And they shall become a sign and a wonder on you and your descendants forever" (Deut. 28:45, 46).

The words of Isaiah:

> **... For they have rejected the law of the LORD of hosts, and despised the word of the Holy One of Israel.**

On this account the anger of the LORD has burned against His people ... (Isa. 5:24, 25).

But they rebelled and grieved His Holy Spirit; therefore, He turned Himself to become their enemy, He fought against them (Isa. 63:10).

"Thus I shall judge you, like women who commit adultery or shed blood are judged; and I shall bring on you the blood of wrath and jealousy. ..." (Ezek. 16:38)

From Daniel and Hosea:

> **"Indeed all Israel has transgressed Thy law and turned aside, not obeying Thy voice; so the curse has been poured out on us, along with the oath which is written in the law of Moses the servant of God, for we have sinned against Him. ..." (Dan. 9:11)**

Listen to the word of the LORD, O sons of Israel, For the LORD has a case against the inhabitants of the land, because there is no faithfulness or kindness or knowledge of God in the land.

There is swearing, deception, murder, stealing, and adultery. They employ violence, so that bloodshed follows bloodshed (Hos. 4:1, 2).

And on and on and on. Believe me, no anti-Semite ever needed the New Testament if he meant to build a case against Israel. But the anti-Semite shows himself a fool by leaving out the other "half" of the Old and New Testaments. True, Israel has sinned and sinned greatly (just like the rest of humanity), but God has promised to redeem her from her sins hundreds of times.

> **"Behold, days are coming," declares the LORD, "when I will make a new covenant with the house of Israel ...**
>
> **"... for they shall all know Me, from the least of them to the greatest of them ... for I will forgive their iniquity, and their sin I will remember no more" (Jer. 31:31, 34).**

This message is repeated from Genesis to Malachi. In fact, it is the theme of the Bible. To miss this great central truth of the Tanach means that one must be spiritually blind and rebellious toward the Word of God.

Likewise, the New Testament is not by any stretch of the imagination anti-Semitic. It, too, preaches that God loves Israel and will restore her. Remember the verses we quoted from Peter's sermon to his Jewish brethren on the day of Shavuot (Pentecost)?

The anti-Semite forgets to quote the rest of the sermon.

> **Now when they heard *this*, they were pierced to the heart, and said to Peter and the rest of the apostles, "Brethren, what shall we do?"**
>
> **And Peter *said* to them, "Repent, and let each of you be baptized in the name of Yeshua the Messiah for the forgiveness of your sins; and you shall receive the gift of the Holy Spirit.**
>
> **"For the promise is for you and your children, and for all who are far off, as many as the Lord our God shall call to Himself" (Acts 2:37-39).**

Note that the 3,000 Jews who listened to Peter and ultimately repented were not offended by Peter's preaching. Rather, they were brought to repentance.

Secondly, Peter told them that God's promise of salvation is first to them — the Jewish nation. Perhaps one could make a case for Peter being anti-Gentile!

Again, we see Peter repeating the same theme in Acts 3. He explains the sin of Israel concerning Yeshua but then says,

> **"And now, brethren, I know that you acted in ignorance, just as your rulers did also.**
>
> **"But the things which God announced beforehand by the mouth of all the prophets, that His Messiah should suffer, He has thus fulfilled.**
>
> **"Repent therefore and return, that your sins may be wiped away, in order that times of refreshing may come from the presence of the Lord ...**
>
> **"For you first, God raised up His Servant, and sent Him to bless you by turning every one *of you* from your wicked ways" (Acts 3:17-19, 26).**

Paul, who has been accused of being against the Jews, gave as clear a promise of redemption as is found in the entire Bible.

For I do not want you, brethren, to be uninformed of this mystery, lest you be wise in your own estimation, that a partial hardening has happened to Israel until the fullness of the Gentiles has come in;

and thus all Israel will be saved; just as it is written, "THE DELIVERER WILL COME FROM ZION, AND HE WILL REMOVE UNGODLINESS FROM JACOB."

"AND THIS IS MY COVENANT WITH THEM, WHEN I TAKE AWAY THEIR SINS."

From the standpoint of the gospel they are enemies for your sake, but from the standpoint of God's choice they are beloved for the sake of the fathers;

for the gifts and the calling of God are irrevocable (Rom. 11:25-29).

These verses, which reveal Israel's sins and punishment, are not anti-Semitic because they were spoken and written by men of Israel who passionately loved their people. It was Paul who said:

I am telling the truth in Messiah, I am not lying, my conscience bearing me witness in the Holy Spirit,

that I have great sorrow and unceasing grief in my heart.

For I could wish that I myself were accursed, *separated* from Messiah for the sake of my brethren, my kinsmen according to the flesh,

who are Israelites ... (Rom. 9:1-4).

What kind of anti-Semite is that? Besides Paul, the only other man in the Bible who offered to be cut off from God for the sake of His people was Moses (Ex. 32:32). What love could be so great as to even entertain the thought of being eternally separated from God for someone else?

Only ignorance would cause a Gentile to think that the Old Testament is anti-Semitic or a Jew to believe that the New Testament is anti-Semitic. Both were written by Israelites (with the possible exceptions of Job, Esther and Luke) who, inspired by God, wrote the words of warning and of a glorious solution for the Jew first and also for the Gentile.

Why Then Are Some Christians Anti-Semitic? How Can They Have the Truth if They Despise Jews?

I am going to address this very complicated subject quite briefly. I was asked this very question on Israeli radio in 1973, after my house had been firebombed by fanatical Orthodox Jews.

I answered the radio reporter, "If an Orthodox Jew comes and bombs my house, do I blame the God of Israel? If a Muslim terrorist kills in the name of God (the Muslims claim they serve the same one and only God the Jews serve), do I blame God? If Gentiles kill six million Jews in the Holocaust, expel millions of Jews from Christian Spain, or create untold catastrophes under the Christian czars in Russia — all in the name of Jesus (Yeshua) or Christianity — can I blame Yeshua?"

Can I blame God for any sin Israel has committed? Can I blame Yeshua for any sins the Gentiles have committed? The question doesn't have to be answered. God can and will be responsible for His own Words found in the Bible. Yeshua is responsible for what is recorded in the New Testament. What wicked men have done in anyone's name, only they themselves are responsible for. And they will be judged for their actions on the day of judgment by God.

Isn't Paul the Creator of Christianity?

It is commonly taught in the Israeli public school system that Yeshua was a good man, a pious rabbi who kept the Jewish law and served His Jewish people. He was then crucified by Romans for advocating revolutionary actions. Afterwards came Paul, who promoted a new religion and made Yeshua into a "god." It is Paul, then, who is to blame for this error.

Firstly, Yeshua Himself said He was the Messiah. To the Samaritan woman who, though not a Jewess, was looking for the Jewish Messiah, Yeshua declared "... I who speak to you am *He*" (Jn. 4:26).

Again when Yeshua's close friend Lazarus died, his sister Martha told Yeshua, "... I have believed that You are the Messiah, the Son of God, *even* He who comes into the world ..." (Jn. 11:27). Upon that confession, Yeshua raised Lazarus from the dead.

One day Yeshua asked his disciples, "Who do you say that I am?" Peter replied, "Thou art the Messiah, the Son of the living God." And Yeshua answered and said, "Blessed are you, Simon Barjona, because flesh and blood did not reveal *this* to you, but My Father who is in heaven" (Matt. 16:15-17). He clearly spoke of Himself as being God and equal with God: Yeshua said to them, "Truly, truly I say to you, before Abraham was born, I am" (Jn. 8:58).

He said it explicitly enough that "... the Jews were seeking ... to kill Him, because He not only was breaking the Sabbath (by healing someone), but also was calling God His own Father, making Himself equal with God" (Jn. 5:18).

In yet another incident, the Jews answered Him, "For a good work we do not stone You, but for blasphemy; and because You, being a man, make Yourself out *to be* God" (Jn. 10:33).

The first public witness to proclaim Yeshua was John the Baptist. As Yeshua's elder, he declared:

> **"... 'He who comes after me has a higher rank than I, for He existed before me'" (Jn. 1:15).**

Matthew and Luke, who were disciples of Yeshua, both proclaimed that Yeshua was born without a human father — that is, without a human sexual act. Instead, God created a baby in a Jewish virgin's womb. If God could create Adam out of dust and Eve out of a rib, obviously He could create Yeshua without a human father.

This was in fulfillment of the words of Moses that the child of a *woman* would crush the head of the evil serpent who brought sin into the world (Gen. 3:15).

Yeshua Himself said, "I and the Father are one" (Jn. 10:30).

> **"I am the way, and the truth, and the life; no one comes**

to the Father, but through Me ..." (Jn. 14:6).

I do not have an exact understanding of God, His Spirit, His Son or how these facets of God's essence interrelate. But one thing I can say for certain to Jewish people: Do not ever let someone tell you that Yeshua was only a nice Orthodox rabbi who was minding His own business until Paul came along.

Either Yeshua is Who He said He is — the Son of God, the Messiah, the Savior of the world, the Lamb of God who takes away the sin of the world — or He is a liar, a fraud and a charlatan. There is no middle ground on this issue. Each person must decide in his heart whether or not he will accept Yeshua as the way, the truth and the life.

Is It Not True That Yeshua Came to the Jews, but Paul Changed Yeshua's Teachings into a Gentile Religion?

The above concept is also taught in Israeli government schools. Of course, textbooks on religious subjects are written primarily by the Orthodox sector. But let us examine Paul's life and actions in light of the Tanach.

We are back to the basic principles of why God originally created Israel. God's original promise to Abraham included: "... And in you all the families of the earth shall be blessed" (Gen. 12:3).

Some people believe that this Scripture was fulfilled in its entirety when Yeshua shed His blood in atonement for our sins. That certainly is the central ingredient. But Yeshua's death alone cannot fulfill in totality that promise to Abraham.

Let us ask ourselves: Have all peoples in the world already been blessed through Abraham? A resounding "No." For until they have heard the Gospel through a human agent, the world cannot know that the blessing exists. Look closely at these Scriptures:

And the Scripture, foreseeing that God would justify the Gentiles by faith, preached the gospel beforehand to Abraham, saying,

"ALL THE NATIONS SHALL BE BLESSED IN YOU" (Gal. 3:8).

For "WHOEVER WILL CALL UPON THE NAME OF THE LORD WILL BE SAVED."

> **How then shall they call upon Him in whom they have not believed? And how shall they believe in Him whom they have not heard? And how shall they hear without a preacher?**
>
> **And how shall they preach unless they are sent? ... (Rom. 10:13-15).**

So the nations could not be blessed without Yeshua dying for their sins *and* Israel proclaiming the news to Gentiles throughout the earth.

The prophets consistently declared that the God of Israel is the God of all the world. For centuries Orthodox Judaism has turned inward. They say, "Leave us alone, and we will leave you alone!" As Orthodox Jews, they have no desire whatsoever to take the news of the one and only God to the world. In effect, they are saying that their God is a provincial God — a local God for the Jews. It is not important to them that all of God's creation turn to Him and believe in Him.

The prophets thought the opposite:

> **"... And there is no other God besides Me, a righteous God and a Savior; there is none except me.**
>
> **"Turn to Me, and be saved, all the ends of the earth; for I am God, and there is no other. ..." (Isa. 45:21, 22).**

"For the sake of Jacob my servant, and Israel My chosen *one* ...

"That men may know from the rising to the setting of the sun that there is no one besides Me. I am the LORD, and there is no other" (Isa. 45:4, 6).

Then it will come about in that day that the nations will resort to the root of Jesse, who will stand as a signal for the peoples; and His resting place will be glorious (Isa. 11:10).

How does Israel become the promised blessing? The principle given in the Bible is that when a person/nation repents, it will automatically become a light, a witness and a bearer of good tidings to others. When

King David, forefather of the Messiah, sinned his great sin, he repented and asked God to forgive him.

Wash me thoroughly from my iniquity, and cleanse me from my sin. ...

Restore to me the joy of Thy salvation ...

***Then* I will teach transgressors Thy ways, and sinners will be turned back to Thee (Psa. 51:2, 12, 13).**

When Israel as a whole returns to God and receives the Lord's atonement for sin, she will naturally be bursting to share this wonderful news with the rest of the world.

This is most certainly what happened to the early Jewish followers of Yeshua and to Paul. They were saved and redeemed by the mighty hand of God. Their sins were covered by the blood of Yeshua. Paul and the early Jewish apostles went out and did exactly what the prophets said they should and would do. They became a light in their own nation and to the known world. They spread the Good News of the God of Israel, fulfilling the purpose for which God chose Israel.

I believe that, because the nation of Israel as a whole did not turn to God 2,000 years ago and fulfill her duty to be a light to the nations, the Christian church lost much valuable teaching and experience to be found in the rich Jewish "root of the olive tree" (Rom. 11:17). As more Jews are saved, they will add a significant fresh richness to the collective body of believers.

No, it was not and is not God's plan for all Gentile believers to become Jews. God is much more a God of variety than that. He said that in His Kingdom will be those "... from every nation and *all* tribes and peoples and tongues ..." (Rev. 7:9). How unfathomable it is that we will one day fellowship in God's Kingdom with redeemed ones from Hawaii, China, Brazil, Siberia, Zaire, Alaska, Argentina and Nigeria! So yes, God is the God of the Gentiles, too. However, it is still our contention that the true Gentile body of believers has suffered loss because of the sin and backsliding of Israel.

I believe that one reason God has been so severe with Israel for falling away from God and remaining in darkness is because she also failed to be the light to the nations. This has been God's destiny for her from the beginning. So, many Gentiles born over the last 2,000 years will come to the judgment day of the Lord as pagans, rather than the redeemed of the Lord, because Israel went her own way. How tragic! (Of course, the same is true of every Gentile who failed to fulfill the call of God on his life.)

Nevertheless, we, both Jews and Gentiles, must be eternally grateful that Jews like Paul and the other apostles committed their lives to obeying the commission of Israel's prophets — to let the world know that "I am God and there is no other."

One day, the prophets promise, a new generation of Jews will pick up where Paul left off:

> **"'And it will come about that just as you were a curse among the nations, O house of Judah and house of Israel, so I will save you that you may become a blessing. ...'" (Zech. 8:13)**

This book is by no means an exhaustive study of questions often asked by Jewish people. Satan has thrown many obstacles in the way of the chosen people to receiving their Messiah. It is his evil plan to make God's Word return void, because the Lord has solemnly promised to redeem His people from their sins.

We, both Jewish and Gentile believers, are God's instruments of redemption. It is we who must proclaim salvation and say to Zion, "Your God reigns!" (Isa. 52:7). If you will ask the Lord for the same love that Yeshua had for His brethren, you can touch the hearts of the lost sheep of Israel.